Connections

Intermediate

TEACHER

Suzanne Carter * Dorothy Woods

1

English Anywhere Inc.
6513 Patricia Avenue
Plano, Texas 75023

www.englishanywhere.org

ISBN-13: 978-1517173159

ISBN-10: 1517173159

Acknowledgements

As the need for speaking English becomes a world wide necessity, the teachers of English are faced with many choices for good curriculum. These lessons are the basic knowledge that students need to begin their acquisition of the English language. Our goal is to provide a structured textbook that can be used by teachers and students to accomplish the skills necessary to speak English as a native speaker. The lessons are designed to aid the student in the spoken language and assume that they have already mastered some of the reading and writing skills taught in many schools around the world.

We have incorporated the most current teaching techniques for acquiring a language, and use many activities to aid in practicing the skills taught in each lesson. In Lesson 12 we included a story and use Penny Hiller's Story Approach to teach the skills needed in that lesson. We have employed the basic concepts of Gardner's *Theory of Multiple Intelligences* to reach the widest range of student's learning, and we hope you will enjoy teaching these lessons.

Special thanks to:

Gloria Ormiston for field testing these lessons in Enable Learning Center in Minneapolis, Minnesota and in the church in Bangkok, Thailand.

Ed Woods for the many hours of contributions and help with these lessons at Enable Learning Center in Minneapolis, Minnesota.

Frank Fitzgerald for helping in the ESL classes at Southern Hills Baptist Church, Tulsa, Oklahoma.

Charles and Yoke Fong Harvey for the support of Grace Ministries and the encouragement they gave as we taught the lessons in Krasang, Thailand.

All of our friends and families who have given their financial, prayer, and spiritual support throughtout the long process of writing and field testing this curriculum.

About the Authors

Suzanne Carter (Texas)

Suzanne is founder and director of English Anywhere, and is retired from teaching elementary school for 33 years. She has been teaching English as Second Language (ESL) for the past 16 years in the USA and in many foreign countries. She has also trained many church volunteers and missionaries to teach ESL curriculum as they seek to serve in their communities. She earned her Bachelor of Science in Education degree from the University of Tulsa, and she got her TESOL certification from Oxford Seminars. She has one daughter. She is currently teaching 4 ESL classes in Texas and training TESOL at the Graduate Institute of Applied Linguistics in Dallas.

Dorothy A. Woods (New York)

Dorothy has served alongside her husband, Edward, as church planters with Continental Baptist Missions since 1970. She has a graduate degree in education and a wide variety of teaching experience. Since 1994, the Lord has privileged Ed and Dorothy to focus on ESL (English as a Second Language) as an outreach of the local church. They have conducted tutor training workshops in churches and Bible colleges in the US, Canada, and overseas. Currently the Woods are living in Minneapolis, where they teach ESL through the Enable Learning Center to Hmong refugees, assist international students at the University of Minnesota, and continue to challenge and equip Christians for Great Commission living. The Woods have three grown children and three grandsons.

Illustrations:

Victor Zamora (Mexico)

Victor is Academic Director for Instituto Blas Pascal. He has taught English for over 12 years to children and adults. He illustrated the Good Neighbor story in Lesson 11.

Cover designed by:

Cynthia Reed (Oklahoma)

Cynthia is the graphics designer and owner of Cynpro Professional Solutions.

Overview

Connections is a conversational English curriculum with an overview of the Bible. It is designed to be used in long term classes lasting 9 months or longer. The format is conversation driven, and it is created to get students speaking from the first lesson. This is a whole language approach working from conversations to break down various sentences, phrases and sound studied in each lesson. The lessons start with a **Theme Picture** to discover any preknowledge students have and set the tone of the lesson. Then the **Conversations** are taught with the vocabulary being taught in the context of the conversations. Next we work on specific sounds and the rhythms of the of the English language in the **Pronunciation** and **Rhythm** segments. Finally, there is a section that discusses a **Bible** lesson. There are 2 parts to each lesson and many activities to give diversity to the English practice.

Recommended books for the lessons are:

A Look Inside America
by Bill Perry
ISBN 0-9633645-5-3

Word by Word Basic Picture Dictionary
by Steven J. Molinsky and Bill Bliss
ISBN 0-13-200355-4

Recommended videos:
"The Hope"
by Mars Hill Productions Inc.
Mars-Hill.org
ISBN 1-892271-02-8

"The God Story"
Produced by the Jeremiah Team
god-story.org

Activities, Strategies, Games, Songs/Chants

Activities, games, chants and songs are **essential** for teaching language. They are the medium through which students practice using the language. Without practice, students will never produce the sounds necessary to communicate. Practice is the core of language learning and communication.

Activites, games, chants and songs are used throughout each lesson for the following reasons:
* to help make learning fun,
* to reinforce all the learning segments,
* to establish true comprehension of new words and phrases, and
* to increase the learning curve by helping students remember up to 90% of the lesson content as opposed to only 20% when passively involved in the lesson by only reading and listening.

There are many wonderful activities included in the lessons. Therefore, appropriate activities have been selected for each lesson and listed in the context of the lessons page. If your students are having difficulty or appear bored with one of the activities listed, switch to one of the others that focuses on the same English topic. Be careful to choose wisely. Also, be careful to always look for every opportunity to get your students talking--by repeating you, teaching a particular point themselves and practicing the conversations, as well as actively participating in the coordinated activities.

Listed below are different kinds of materials needed for the activities, plus some of the prep work needed. Very little extra is required, with the exception of gathering good pictures. These are <u>very important</u>. We have provided a book of "Teaching Charts and Pictures", to save the teacher time and printing costs.

Materials:
Pictures, flashcards, blank index cards, bean bags, soft balls, chart paper for maps, markers, real maps, blank paper and pencils, minimal props for teaching the stories and certain vocabulary words, plastic sleeves for protection of pictures

Preparation:
1. Collect good pictures that very specifically show the word you are teaching, with few or no other objects in the picture unless necessary to convey what the vocabulary word is. See the Teaching Charts and Pictures for the things you need.
2. For good presentation of pictures and help in playing games, either place each picture in a plastic sleeve backed with a sheet of colored or construction paper or mount the pictures on construction paper or index cards.
3. Make vocabulary and/or number flashcards for certain activities. We have suggested activities and <u>Materials</u> to gather before each lesson.

Table of Contents

Theme Picture

The Theme Picture may be used to start the theme discussion for the lesson or as a basis for review.

Teaching steps:
1. Ask the students, "What do you see?"
2. Focus the students on the theme of the lesson. This gives them an opportunity to switch their thinking to English.
3. Do not rush but allow time for them to think of English words to discuss what they see. It takes time for people to start thinking in a new language so a warm-up or review time is important. Encourage "English only" during the lesson to keep the students focused.
4. Repeat the names of things the students identify and show the rest of the class.
5. Use the article (a, an, the) with nouns.
6. If students want to see the words, write them on a board, using lower case letters, unless a word should be capitalized.

Example:

> Higher Level
>
> A man and a woman are shaking hands.
>
> The man in the middle is introducing them.
>
> The woman has glasses.

Objectives

1. Students will be able to ask for and give orally and written personal information. (name, address, phone #, & family)
2. Show understanding and answer "what" questions asked in a basic interview.
3. Read and write numbers using the appropriate patterns and forms. (social security #, phone #, address #)
4. Interpret and complete simple forms using personal information.
5. Show ability to greet people formally and informally.

Materials Needed for Lesson 1

1. Paper and pens (Sign In chart)
2. Pictures to illustrate all of the vocabulary
3. Pronunciation and Rhythm charts
4. Song chart - globe ball
5. Name tags for students and teachers
6. "Hot Seat" forms

1　Greetings & Introductions

Creation

Conversations

Part 1
Conversation 1
Greeting

A. <u>Hello.</u> How are you?
B. <u>Fine</u> thank you. And you?
A. <u>Fine</u>. Thank you.

(Discuss: Why do you want to learn to speak English?)

 Conversations

The conversations in the curriculum are intended to provide a framework for basic social communiation. The framework consists of forms, or patterns, into which many words (parts of speech) can be substituted to enable students to speak English quickly, not just learn vocabulary.

This is a conversation that you will hear young people use. You can add special conversations your students need, making sure they fit the reality of your students. Remember that students not only need to understand English but also need their spoken English to be understood.

Idiom:

A. <u>Hey.</u> What's up?
B. Not much. You?
A. Do you wanna (want to) hang out?
B. Sure. Whatcha wanna do? (What do you want to do?)

Teaching steps:
1. **Model the conversation several times**, using your partner or one of your students. Use A and B cards to indicate the dual parts.

2. **Act out the main vocabulary words of the conversation as you teach.** This is teaching vocabulary naturally in context. Some of the vocabulary words are on the **Vocabulary** page; others must be memorized in the context of the conversation, as all words cannot be translated literally. Quickly involve the students. Check comprehension by having students act the words out themselves, coaching them until they are confident. Listen for good pronunciation and rhythm. The objective is for the students to be understood.

* Substitution Drill: Substitute words for <u>hello</u> and <u>fine.</u>

Substitute these words for <u>hello.</u>
* hi
* hey

Substitute these for "How are you?"
* How are you doing?
* What's goin' on?
* How ya been?
* Whatcha been doin' lately?

These may be substituted for "Fine thank you."
* I'm fine, thanks.
(Thank you is often shortened to "thanks".)
* I'm good.
* I feel great.
* I feel wonderful.
* Super!
* Can't complain.
* Everything's cool.

These may also be substituted for "Fine thank you."
* I'm sad.
* I'm bummed.
* Not so good.
* I'm okay.

Discussion:

In a formal setting just use Conversation 1 as a greeting and go on to other topics. In a more informal setting with friends, you may actually discuss how you are doing. Act out both settings with students so they understand the difference.

Formal Greetings

Informal Greetings

hang out

hang out (hanging out, hangin' out, hang)
To spend your time idly or lounging about, spending time with friends

Act this out with the students.

Part 1

Conversation 2

> A. Hello, my name is _____ ___. What's your name?
>   * I'm _____. What's your name?
> B. I'm _(name)_.
> A. It's nice to meet you.
>   * It's good to meet you.
>   * It's a pleasure to meet you.
>   * I'm happy to meet you.
> B. It's nice to meet you, too.

Follow the same teaching steps used in Conversation 1 each time you introduce a new conversation.

Be sure to listen carefully to your higher level students. Each word said is important. Listen for the "c" in "nice" and the "t" at the end of "meet".

Always correct mistakes by modeling the correct use of the word(s) in the context of a sentence. Then have the student repeat the correct sentence. Check to see if the student has understood by having him/her use the challenging word(s) in another sentence. Give more explanations of how to use the words if others in the class need this; otherwise, have the student see you after class. If the problem persists, look for a good activity that will help the students practice this by using a lot of body motions, songs or chants, or use as many of the five senses as possible.

happy
glad
nice
great
wonderful
pleasure

C A B

Conversation 3

A. __(Name) (B)__ , this is my <u>wife</u> __(name)(C)__.
B. <u>Nice</u> to meet you.
   * I've heard wonderful things about you.
   * Your husband has told me great things about you.
C. <u>Nice to meet you, too</u>.
   * I'm glad to meet you, too.

For formal introductions in a social setting you begin by introducing yourself. You may not have to ask the person their name since it is implied that you want to know their name. There are several polite responses.

When introducing two adults; friend to a relative, a woman to a man, an older person to a younger person follow this order. However, the order is not critical. The introduction is usually followed by giving some information about the two people you are introducing.
Example:
   After introducing your wife to a colleague, you might say,
        "We work in the same office."

a girlfriend - a boyfriend
a fiancé (a man who is engaged)
a fiancée (a woman)
a wife
a husband

a friend (friends)
a pal (pals)
a buddy (buddies)
a colleague (colleagues)
    -a co-worker
an aquaintance (review use of "an")

13

 **Pronunciation**

Part 1

f	**b**	**m**	**a**
fine	**b**oyfriend	**m**an	**a**nd
feel	**b**uddy	**m**eet	ha**n**d
fiancé	**b**ud	**m**e	husba**n**d
fiancée	**b**ummed	**m**y	ma**n**
friend	***b**eginning	**m**uch	has
for	***b**irds	***m**oon	gla**d**
***f**irst		***m**inute	ha**pp**y
***f**ourth		***m**ay	***a**nimals
***f**ifth		***m**essage	*m**a**n
***f**ish			*wom**a**n
			*l**a**nd

h	**w**	**t**	**i (long)**
husband	**w**onderful	**t**o	n**i**ce
hey	**w**ife	**t**oday	h**i**
heard	**w**orld	**t**omorrow	w**i**fe
how	**w**hat's	**t**ogether	**I**'m
happy	***w**hen	**T**uesday	**i**dly
w**h**ole	***w**oman	**t**alking	m**y**
hang out	***w**as	**t**ime	
		take	

*The asterisks indicate the words for Part 2

Pronunciation

This segment helps students start to sound more like native English speakers. Most of the words used in this segment are words introduced in the lesson, previous lessons or words that are very common. Therefore, it is not necessary to take the time to explain the meaning of any words while teaching pronunciation.

It is extremely important to use your natural pronunciation, tone of voice and speed when teaching this segment. Practice the words ahead of time to be sure you are using the correct sound, especially for vowels. Remember to say the sound of the letter rather than its name.

Most of the English sounds are "voiced", which means the vocal chords vibrate when the letter is pronounced. However, there are some "unvoiced" sounds:
/f/ /h/ /p/ /s/ /t/ /x/ /sh/ /ch/ /wh/ and /th/. (There is also a voiced /th/ sound.) Unvoiced sounds do not use the vocal chords. Air is forced out of the mouth in a short burst.

When pronouncing each sound, be sure to pronounce only the letter itself. Do not add a vowel to it, such as /ba/ instead of /b/.

Teaching steps:
1. Put the sound and example words on the board or use a prepared chart. Teach only one column at a time, using **Model, Repeat, Solo (MRS)** for each column before going to the next.

2. **Model:** Say the sound several times while pointing to it.
   /b/ /b/ /b/
   Then say the sound and quickly read the entire list, pointing to each word as you read it.
   /b/ baby, babies, book, bee, big
   <u>Students just watch and listen.</u>

3. **Repeat:** Say the sound and each column of words several times as your students repeat the sound and column of words. Be sure to use your normal voice and rate of speed. Beware of "singing" the column like a list of items by thinking of each word as a separate sentence. Drop your voice at the end of each word as though there is a period there. Do one column at a time.

4. **Solo:** Have the whole class say the sound and the words in the column by themselves. Then have small groups of students solo, say the words by themselves, and then have individuals say them.

   Give lots of encouragement and praise!

Part 1

thank you
boyfriend
girlfriend
pretty
super
pleasure
husband
colleague
lounging
spending
*****spe**cial

he**llo**
good-**bye**
hang **out**
o**kay**
com**plain**
a**bout**
what's **up**
to**day**
*a **man**
*the **earth**

wonderful
everything
idly
hangin' out
Saturday
*****holy** day

to**geth**er
fi**an**cé
*be**gin**ning
*cre**at**ed
*the **hea**vens
*have **chil**dren
*the **wo**man
*to**mor**row

*The asterisks indicate the words for Part 2

Rhythm

This segment will help your students with accent reduction. It is essential that you use your natural stress, rhythm and intonation patterns throughout the segment and the entire lesson. This exercise teaches only the primary stress of a word. If the primary stresses are correct, students are more likely to be understood, whether or not their secondary or tertiary stresses are correct.

Each dot stands for a syllable. The large dot is the primary stress.

Teaching steps:

1. Put the stress dots and example words on the board as they appear in the lesson or use a prepared chart. Teach only one column at a time, using **Model, Repeat, Solo** for each column before going to the next.

2. Clap, slap or tap the rhythm of the stress pattern to be taught. Clap loudly for the big dots and softly (or not at all) for the small dots. Begin the clapping, and after everyone is in unison, say the words in that column as you continue clapping, slapping or tapping. As you **model** the rhythm, don't slow down or drag the pace. If you have to slow down because your students can't keep up, then do so, but return to a normal pace as soon as possible.

3. For Basic Level students, say each word in the column in time to the rhythm and have them repeat each word after you. Then say the entire column in time to the rhythm and have the students **repeat** the entire column after you.

    For Higher Level students, say the entire column in time to the rhythm and have the students repeat the entire column after you.

4. Have the group say the entire column by themselves and then have individual students say the words by themselves (**solo**).

Teachers may find clapping the rhythm distracting during the solo part. Therefore, students may stop clapping during this part so the teacher can actually hear the placement of the stress in their voices.

Remember the goal is to have the students say the words with correct intonation and syllable stress while having fun!

Activities 🚲

Part 1

Songs

Songs are valuable memory tools to help learn and remember anything of a linguistic nature. Students can learn English words in songs and chants more quickly than most other ways. Repeat songs often and on successive days, and by the end of the week your students leave with a lot of English.

Teaching a song is similar to teaching a conversation or a concept.

Teaching steps:
1. Sing the entire song as learners listen.
2. Then say the words of the song with rhythm and intonation. Note the syllable separation and stress. Discuss the meanings of the vocabulary words they know and those they do not know simultaneously as you teach the lines.
3. Say one line at a time with learners repeating after you. Do this several times.
4. Have learners say the entire song together with rhythm and intonation.
5. Model singing the melody.
6. Have the students sing the song along with you as they gain confidence.

Hot Seat

The **Hot Seat** is an information gathering activity and can be used as a get-acquainted activity. It is also great for practicing the pronouns, "he & she" and the possessive adjectives, "his, her & their".

Paired Hot Seat:
* Pair students, giving them 5 minutes to interview each other.
* When the class comes together again, one pair comes to the front, Students #1 & 2.
* Student #1 sits in a chair in the front of the class, the **Hot Seat**.
* Student #2 stands next to him.
* Student #2 tells the other students what he learned about Student #1.

* Students #1 & 2 trade places.
* Student #1 tells the other students about Student #2.
* The first pair, Pair A, trades places with a second pair, Pair B--Students #3 & 4.
* Continue with the interviewing until every pair has been in the **Hot Seat**.

Song:

He's Got the Whole World in His Hands

1. He's got the whole world in His hands.
   He's got the whole world in His hands.
   He's got the whole world in His hands.
   He's got the whole world in His hands.

He = God

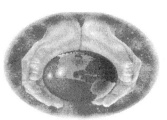

 ## How to teach "He's Got the Whole World in His Hands"

Read through the song with the same rhythm that you sing it.
Use "Backward Build Up" to teach the line.
1. <u>Hands</u> - Hold up your hands and say, "hands".
2. World - Point to a map of the world or a globe and say, "world".
3. Whole - Move your hand around the map or globe and say, "whole".
4. He - Point up and say, "he = God". If your class has no concept of God as a being who is up in heaven, use the native word for God.
5. Now say the whole sentence using the same gestures.
6. Next use the CD or sing the tune using the words you have just taught. Ask students to join in as soon as they can.
7. Sing as many times as you feel necessary, and then add names to the song as indicated in verse 2.

* Verse 2 - Now add names.
      Example: He's got <u>Maria</u> and <u>Chi</u> in His hands.
                He's got Maria and Chi in His hands.
                He's got Maria and Chi in His hands.
                He's got the whole world in His hands.
Keep substituting names until you have put everyone's name in the song.

In subsequent lessons add verses as students become familiar with the melody.   I usually teach one new song per month, and we sing it at the beginning of each teaching session.

 **Bible Lesson**

 Discussion

Discussion is the heartbeat of your lesson. This is where you discover whether or not students are grasping the content of the lesson. The teacher must be patient to allow enough time for the students to think not only of their response but also of the English words that fit the discussion. Do not be quick to jump in and explain concepts, define words or give them an English answer! Remember people only retain about 20% of what they hear but tend to remember up to 70-90% when they are engaged in discussions and activities.

Think about this: You may only remember 10% of what you are reading right now to help you learn how to teach this curriculum. If you participate in a workshop, you may retain 70-90%!!!!!

Discussion questions are provided in the lessons. Feel free to add as much discussion as is appropriate for the student's English level and the time frame.

Discuss the spiritual aspects of the story as much as possible.

Part 1

The Creation

In the beginning God spoke and created the heaven and the earth.

On the first day God spoke and created light. He called the light, Day and the dark, Night. God saw it was good.

On the second day God spoke and created the sky. God saw it was good.

On the third day God spoke and created the land and seas, and the plants. God saw it was good.

On the fourth day God spoke and created the sun, the moon and the stars. God saw it was good.

Taken from Genesis 1:1-2:4.

Discussion Questions:
1. Who created the heavens and the earth?
2. When did God create the heavens and earth?
3. How did God create the heavens and earth?
4. What was created on day 1-4?

In the <u>beginning</u> God <u>spoke</u> and <u>created</u> the <u>heaven</u> and the <u>earth</u>.

      beginning--the first part, start   What is the *beginning*? Is it the beginning of the
              world? time? life? Show a watch or clock to indicate time.
              Write 12:00am as the beinning of a new day.

     God--the Creator, Allow the students to tell their idea of God.

    spoke & created-- Can we "make" something by simply speaking? "Make"
              something in front of the students. Draw a picture, fold a paper airplane,
              etc. Say, "Make" as you are doing it. People can make things out of
              materials, but only God can create from nothing.

     heavens--Point up and show pictures of sky, stars, planets, etc. Say, "Heavens".

     earth--Use a globe or map of the world and say, "Earth".

REVIEW: ordinal numbers

On the first day God created <u>light.</u> He called light, Day and the <u>dark</u>, Night.
   God saw it was <u>good</u>.

     light & dark--Turn the lights off and on several times or use a flashlight. Then turn the
              light on and say, "light". Turn the lights off and say, "dark". Do it several
              times and say, "God made light." Next show pictures of lights and say,
              "God calls the light, Day. Teach these as opposites.
              Use a black piece of paper and say, "God calls dark, Night.

     good--Act out someone helping someone with a heavy load. Say, "Help, good."
              Act out several "good" things and each time emphasize "good".
              Then say, "God saw that it was good." Have students repeat.
              Teadh these as opposites.

On the second day God created the <u>sky</u>.
   God saw it was good.

     sky--Go outside and point up to the sky and say, "sky", or use pictures of the sky.
              Students repeat the sentence,"God saw that it was good."

On the third day God created the <u>land and sea, and the plants.</u>
   God saw it was good.

      land--Show pictures of different kinds of land. MRS "land".
      seas--Show lots of pictures of seas/oceans. MRS "sea".
      plants--Show pictures of different kinds of plants. Talk about categories "trees,
              bushes," etc.Students repeat the sentence, "God saw that it was good."

On the fourth day God created <u>the sun, the moon, and the stars.</u>
   God saw it was good.

     sun, moon, stars - Show pictures of the sun, moon, and stars
           Talk about the placement of each and how the earth is in a perfect
           position in the universe to support life.

    The video called "The Hope" is included with this curriculum.You may
    use it as a preview of what we are going to be studying or show each
    part of it as you work your way through the Bible lessons.

Conversations

Part 2

Review the song from Part 1 "He's got the Whole World in His Hands." Then review the introductions and add informal introductions like this one.

Conversation 1

Informal Greeting

A. <u>Mike,</u> this is my <u>friend</u> <u>Bob</u>.
B. It's great to meet you, man.
   <u>Susan</u> has told me so much about you.

Conversations and Vocabulary:

Remember to teach the vocabulary in the context of the conversations.
Ex: Teach the names of the different people and substitute the vocabulary that fits the situation.
Reinforce the new vocabulary by doing the activity **Substitution Circle.**

Remember this is conversational English, not a traditional English class in school. This should be fun for you and the students. It is not a time for teaching a list of vocabulary words by having students read them, write them and look up definitions. That is literacy. This is learning vocabulary and grammar naturally in typical social conversations.

 Substitution Circle
Have students sit in a circle. Have 3 students stand up and practice introducing one to another. After all three have introduced each other, choose 3 more students, and keep going around the circle until everyone has introduced and been introduced to everyone else.

Conversation 2

Phone Conversations

A. Hello, my name is ___.
  * Hello, this is ___.
  * Hello, I'm ___.
  May I speak to ___?
  * Is ___ home?
  * May I please speak to ___?
B Yes, just a minute please.
  * No, may I take a message?
  * ___ can't come to the phone right
    now. May I take a message?
  * What is your name?
  * What is your phone number?

Telephone conversations are one of the most difficult exercises for students because of the fear that the person with whom they are speaking will say something that they don't understand. If students can learn to write down a name and phone number they can begin feeling confident in answering the phone and can get help if they need to understand the message.
 Review numbers 0-9 with students and make sure they can <u>pronounce</u> them correctly.

Conversation 3

Leaving

A. I have to go now.
  * It's getting late. I have to go.
  * It's time to go.

B. See you later.
  * Talk to you <u>later.</u>
  * I'll see you <u>tomorrow.</u>
  * I'll see you on <u>Sunday.</u>
A. Okay.
  * Sure.
  * It has been good talking to you.
  * It's been good to see you.
  * Let's get together again.
B. Good- bye.
  * Bye.

next <u>Monday</u>
next week
on <u>Tuesday</u>
REVIEW:
days of the week

 Knowing the protocal for leaving is an important skill in any culture. It is good to discuss appropriate ways to leave a social setting, formal and informal. Practice these with your students until they feel comfortable saying each one. This conversation can be used in person or on the phone. Review the days of the week with students and work on any that are hard to pronounce.

Bible Lesson

Part 1

The Creation

In the beginning God spoke and created the heaven and the earth.

On the first day God spoke and created light. He called the light, Day and the dark, Night. God saw it was good.

On the second day God spoke and created the sky. God saw it was good.

On the third day God spoke and created the land and seas, and the plants.   God saw it was good.

On the fourth day God spoke and created the sun, the moon and the stars. God saw it was good.

Part 2

On the fifth day God spoke and created fish and birds. God saw it was good.

On the sixth day God spoke and created land animals. Then He made a man and a woman. God saw it was good.

God told the man and the woman to rule the earth and to have children. God saw it was very good.

On the seventh day God rested. Day seven was a special holy day.

This is how God created the heavens and the earth.

Taken from Genesis 1:1-2:4

Discussion Questions:
Review Part 1
1. Who created the heavens and the earth?
2. When did God create the heavens and earth?
3. How did God create the heavens and earth?
4. What was created on day 1-4?
Part 2
4. What was created on day 5-6?
5. What did God tell the man and woman to do?
6. What did God do on the seventh day?
7. Discuss anything about creation that interests the students. ex. compare evolution & creation.

On the fifth day God created <u>fish and birds</u>. God saw it was good.

fish & birds - Show as many pictures of different species as you can.

On the sixth day God created <u>land animals, a man and a woman</u>. God saw it was good.

land animals - Show as many pictures to illustrated the different species.

man & woman - Use real objects this time "a man" and "a woman".

Be sure to check for comprehension each time you introduce something new by going back to previous pictures/things and asking, "What is this?" Also check by intentionally making mistakes. For example, point to a woman and ask, "Is this a man?" Point to a picture of a fish and ask, "Is this a bird?'

God told the man and the woman to <u>rule</u> the earth and to have children. God saw it was <u>very</u> good.

rule--to have authority over, take care of

very--extremely

Talk about the fact that God told them to have children before sin entered the world.

On the seventh day God <u>rested</u>. Day seven was a <u>special</u> <u>holy</u> day.

rested--Act out the concepts, eg. "God rested." Lay down and say, "rest".

special--honor, respect for, a day set apart to rest

holy--pure, divine

This is how God created the heavens and the earth.

* Tell students to do something. (Write your name on this paper. Then have a helper shrug their shoulders and say, "How?' Then show them "how" to write their name on the paper.)

Discussion: Did God rest because he was tired? Because he was through creating? What do <u>you</u> think of God?

Song:

1. He's Got the Whole World in His Hands

He = God

He's got the whole world in His hands.
He's got the whole world in His hands.
He's got the whole world in His hands.
He's got the whole world in His hands.

More verses:

2. He's got <u>the heaven and earth</u> in His hands.
   He's got <u>the light and the dark</u> in His hands.
   He's got <u>the sky and the land</u> in His hands.
   He's got the whole world in His hands.

3. He's got <u>the seas and the plants</u> in His hands.
   He's got <u>the sun, moon, and stars</u> in His hands.
   He's got <u>the animals and man</u> in His hands.
   He's got the whole world in His hands.

4. On the seventh day He rested from all His work.(sing 3X)
   He's got the whole world in His hands.

Objectives

Students will be able to:

1. Ask for and give oral and written personal information about their family, work and education.
2. Show understanding and answer "what" questions asked in a basic interview.
3. Read, write and pronounce numbers.
4. Demonstrate abililty to ask and answer "where" questions.

Materials Needed for Lesson 2

1. Paper and pens - Sign In chart
2. Pictures to illustrate all of the vocabulary, a jar of dirt
3. Pronunciation and Rhythm charts
4. Song chart - from Lesson 1
5. Name tags for students and teachers
6. Pictures of your own family
7. Number cards & a bean bag
8. 10 index cards with X on 5 and O on 5 cards
9. Matching cards for Consentration

2   Family

The First Family

 Follow the steps for the Theme Picture

Part 1

Conversation 1

> A. Who is this?
> B. This is <u>a family</u>. (a grandfather, an uncle, etc.)
> A. Who are these?
> B. These are my <u>cousins.</u> (nieces, nephews, etc.)

* Use the theme picture and the vocabulary pictures to have a discussion of the family words. Put in the various family words. Each time the teacher should ask "Who is this?" The students answer, "This is a ___ ." (MRS)

Conversation 2

> A. I'm <u>a mother</u>.
> B. I'm <u>a father</u>.

Substitution Circle:

* Get your students into a circle.
* Go around the circle having each student say, "I am a _____."
  (Go around several times, each time using a different family word.)
* Then, looking or pointing to another student, say,
    "You are a _____."
* Go around the circle with each student pointing to another student and
    looking directly at them, saying, "You are a _____."
* Then look at one person but point to another and say,
    "He/She is a _____."
* Continue around the circle with each student taking a turn.

For plurals:
   * Point to yourself and some others and say, "We are _____."
       (mothers/women)
   * Go around the circle with each student taking a turn.
   * Have each student point to two other students saying,
       "You are _____."
   * Point to 2 or more different students and tell the group,
       "They are _____."
   * Go around the circle having each student taking a turn.
For higher levels:
   * Challenge higher level students with more complicated sentences.
       For example, have students make compound sentences,
       "I am a mother but she is not." "I am a mother, and he is a father."

Who is this? This is a ____.
Who are these? These are ____.

an uncle
(uncles)

a grandfather   a grandmother
(grandfathers)   (grandmothers)

an aunt
(aunts)

a niece
(nieces)

a nephew
(nephews)

a grandson
(grandsons)

a granddaughter
(granddaughters)

a nephew
(nephews)

a cousin
(cousins)

a niece
(nieces)

 This lesson starts working on pronouns: I, you, he, she, we, they.
Using them in the context of family discussion teaches pronouns
naturally and shows how to use them in conversation.

Married: having a spouse--a husband or wife
My grandfather is married to my grandmother.
My father is not married to my mother. They are divorced.

a mother-in-law	a stepmother	baby = under 1 year, youngest
a father-in-law	a stepfather	a kid = a child, a young person
a son-in law	a stepson	(kids = children, young people)
a daughter-in-law	a stepdaughter	teenager = 13 years - 19 years

29

Conversations

Conversation 3

A. John, this is my family.

B. Who are these people?
A. They're my <u>grandparents</u>. *(brothers, cousins)*

B. Who is this person?
A. He is my <u>stepson</u>. *(kid brother, nephew.)*

B. Who is that person?
A. She is my <u>niece</u>. *(aunt, baby sister.)*

* Bring pictures of your family and discuss family words with them.
* Ask students to bring pictures of their own family for the next session.
* Never Ending Story is a good activity to do with this lesson.

Never Ending Story using pronouns and possessive adjectives:
   Use all the pronouns and the possessive adjectives" *my* and *your*", plus any others the students know. You may want to draw the pictures together first and then break into pairs to discuss. Draw yourself and your family first, and then add to the picture as it applies to you.   Walk around the class assisting and coaching. Make teaching points to the entire class when you find problems most of the students have in common.
Example:

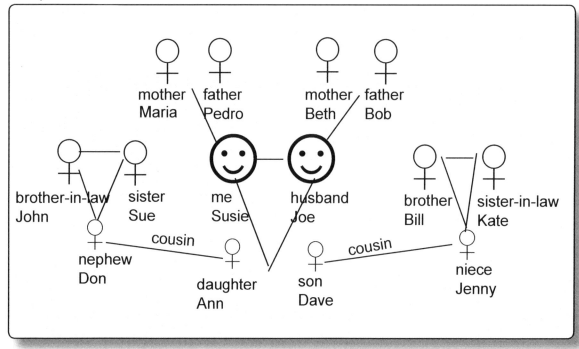

Never Ending Story

The **Never Ending Story** fosters fluency, vocabulary building, creativity and teamwork. It is a way to draw or tell a story in class. This process can be done individually or in groups, in separate sessions, or as an on-going activity. It could be useful for part of the class to work on while the teacher is working with others; it can also be used as a tool to determine the English level of students.

Set a time limit and see how much can be accomplished by each team/individual. Enjoy the process! It is limited only by the imagination of your students!

There are many different subjects about which students can tell stories. One that works well in any setting is the family.

Student-drawn family pictures:
Give each student a sheet of paper. Students draw pictures of their families to share with the group. Students sit in pairs as though showing family pictures and converse with their partners, telling them about each person. Walk around the class assisting and coaching.

Student: This is my mother.
Partner: What's her name?
Student: Her name is Mary. She cleans houses.
Partner: Where does she work?
Student: She works in people's homes.
Student: This is my father, John. He works in a factory.
Continue in a like manner with all family members.

* The partner then shares his/her family drawing as the student did in the example above. Encourage students to share as much as possible in English.
* Each set of partners now pairs up with another set of partners or simply change partners to share their family drawing with another person.

Pronunciation

Part 1

n
nice
niece
nephew
au**n**t
so**n**
cousi**n**
*childre**n**
*garde**n**
*k**n**owledge

st
stepfather
stepmother
stepson
stepdaughter
stepbrother
stepsister
*du**st**
*fir**st**

gr
grandfather
grandmother
grandson
grand-
  daughter
***gr**eat
*de**gr**ee

u (short)
uncle
co**u**sin
h**u**sband
yo**u**ng
***u**nconscious
***u**nder
***u**nderstand

th(voiced)
the
this
that
these
those
fa**th**er
mo**th**er
bro**th**er
*brea**th**ed
*o**th**er
***th**em

d
day
dark
daughter
divorced
*Lor**d**
*breathe**d**
*marrie**d**
*chil**d**
*worl**d**
***d**ust

l
light
co**ll**eague
gir**l**friend
pa**l**
ho**l**y
midd**l**e
*specia**l**
*wonderfu**l**
*beautifu**l**
*materia**l**

e (long)
m**ee**t
ni**e**ce
th**e**se
t**ee**nager
hol**y**
***E**den
***e**vil
***E**ve

Notice that sometimes there are different letters
that make the phonetic sound.

*The asterisks indicate the words for Part 2

Every time you teach Prounuciation and Rhythm use the same steps that you used in Lesson 1.

hel**lo**
hang **out**
o**kay**
com**plain**
a**bout**
di**vorced**
*a**lone**
*a**live**
*ex**cept**

boyfriend
girlfriend
super
pleasure
happy
husband
spending
lounging
***gar**den
***know**ledge

grandfather
stepmother
stepbrother
stepsister
stepdaughter
son-in-law
teenager
***beau**tiful
***land**scaping

Idioms:

a kid = a child, a
    young person
kids = children or
    young people
chill out (chill)- calm
    down, be quiet

Chill out!

* Choose outgoing students to act out the idioms by playing parts. One is the "kid" who cries and the other is the older child who says, "Chill out!" Be sure to use lots of dialogue while acting this out. Act out as many situations as you can think of where this idiom would be appropriate.

Part 1

Act out or show pictures of as many of the words and concepts as you can rather than merely talk about them.

The First Family

The LORD God made a man from the dust of the ground.
God breathed life into the man and named him Adam.
The LORD put Adam in a garden called Eden and told him to take care of it and name all of the animals.
God placed all kinds of beautiful fruit trees in the garden.
Two special trees were in the middle of the garden.

Definitions:
dust - soil, dirt, loose surface material of the earth; Show the jar of dirt.
breathed - to blow in life giving air; Blow air out.
life - to make alive; as when a baby is born; show pictures
garden - a place with beautiful landscaping; Show pictures of gardens.
Eden - a special garden planned by God
take care of - see about, look after
name all of the animals - Adams first job
placed - put in a specific spot; place several things on the table and each time say, "I placed the ___ on the table. Then have the students do it.
beautiful - pretty, lovely, gorgeous; use the sentence, "___ is beautiful."
fruit trees - bearing fruit of all kinds; show pictures of fruit trees
special - unique, not ordinary: God makes everything special.
middle - center; have 3 students line up. Point to the middle person.
         Say, "middle."

Discussion Questions:
1. How did God create the man?
2. How was it different from the way He created the universe?
3. What did God name the man?
4. Where did He put Adam?
5. What was the garden called?
6. What job did God give Adam?
7. What was in the garden?
8. What was in the middle of the garden?

Part 2

One was a tree that gave life and the other was a tree that gave knowledge of good and evil.
But God said, "You may eat fruit from any tree in the garden except the tree that gives knowledge of good and evil. If you eat of that tree, you will die."
God also said, "It is not good for man to be alone."
So he made Adam go to sleep and He took one of man's ribs and made a woman.
Adam named her Eve.
He told them to have children, and this was the first family.

Taken from Genesis 2

Definitions:
knowledge - knowing, understanding: Point to your head
good - anything having to do with God: Have students tell about something good.
evil - anything that doesn't have to do with God: Have students tell about something bad.
except - not, excluding, other than
die - cease to live: Talk about death and life.
alone - without any companions: Show a picture.
sleep - unconscious: Show a picture.
ribs - bones on each side of the chest: Have students feel their ribs.
Adam - the name God gave the first man
Eve - the name Adam gave to the first woman
first family - Adam, Eve, & children

Discussion Questions:
   1. What were the two special trees?
   2. Why did God tell them NOT to eat of the tree of the knowledge of good and evil?
   3. How did He create a woman? Why?
   4. What did God name her?
   6. What did God tell them to have?
   7. Why is the family important to God?

Once you have discussed the whole story, it would be good to act it out as a final review. Choose students to play the parts; God, Adam, Eve. As you act out each sentence, have all of the students say the sentence. Then go to the next sentence. Each time have everyone say the sentence with you. This involves the students in speaking English and it is a fun activity.

 Close each session with prayer when appropriate. Ask for any prayer requests that your students have.

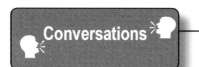

Conversations

Part 2

Questions to ask in a social setting; make sure students answer with complete sentences.

Conversation 1

Family questions:

* Are you married / single?

* Do you have any children / grandchildren?
* How many sons / daughters?
* How old are your children/ grandchildren?
* What does your son / daughter do?

Conversation 2

Work questions:
* Where do you work?
* What do you do?
* How long have you been working there?

Conversation 3

School questions:
* Where do you go to school?
* What are you studying?
* What field are you going into?
* What degree are you working on?
* What is your major?
* What year/level are you?
    Bachelors
        year 1 -freshman
        year 2 -sophomore
        year 3 -junior
        year 4 -senior
    Masters
    Doctorate

Conversation 4

Information questions:
* Where do you work?
* What is your phone number?
* And what is your address?
* What is your email address?
* Do you have a business card?

OCCUPATIONS			DEGREE (MAJOR)
homemaker	lawyer	restaurant	
teacher	mechanic	worker	
welder	plumber	fisherman	Business
engineer	painter	truck driver	Education
construction	computer	factory worker	Engineering
worker	programmer	oil field worker	Science
landscaper	set up	electrician	Mathematics
farmer	technician		Law
doctor	designer		Medical
nurse	policeman		Nursing
secretary	postman		
receptionist	fireman		

 Collect many pictures of people working. Use the pictures in a matching game of Concentration or Tic-Tac-Toe.(See next page.)

Concentration

This game reinforces students' ability to recognize vocabulary words and to make complete sentences with the lesson's vocabulary and grammar.

* Prepare matching cards--2 cards with the same picture, word or number on them.
* Spread the cards out facedown on a table or a flat surface,and mix them up.
* Student #1 turns over a card and identifies it by speaking in a full sentence.
* He then turns over another card, identifies it speaking in a full sentence as well and determines if the 2 match.
* He says either, "This is a match" or "This is not a match."
* If it's a match, he keeps the pair in a stack in front of him.
    (Option: Student #1 can have another turn or not, as you choose.)
* If it's not a match, he turns the cards back over, ending his turn.
* Student #2 proceeds in a like manner.
* Continue around the table until all the matches have been made.
* The winner is the student with the most matches.

Activities

Tic-Tac-Toe

This is an excellent game for any vocabulary exercise. Students can practice simple to complex English--not only simple nouns and sentences but also detailed descriptions. This game can be played with 2 individuals or as teams. Do this as an oral activity, not a literacy one. To save wear and tear on your pictures, place them in plastic sleeves with colored paper behind them.

This game is especially good for team play. It encourages the shy students to speak as their teammates help them figure out the word and strategy of the game.

* On a white board or chart paper, draw lines as shown below.
* Place a vocabulary picture in each of the 9 grids using tape or sticky tack.
* After choosing sides, the goal is for one of the teams/ students to be able to make a row of 3 X's or 3 O's. This can be a row across, down, or diagonal. Players try to block the opponent while trying to make their own row.
* Of course, the first person or team that gets a row of X's or O's is the winner.
* As each person/team chooses a space, they take the picture down and must say, "This is a ___." If they are more advanced have the student describe the picture. Encourage as much dialogue as possible during the game.
* Model the game to make sure students understand how to play. Model a turn for the class. Point to a picture and say. "This is a ___." Then pick up that picture and make an X/O in that grid.
* Have teams/students proceed to play the game in a similar fashion.
* Be sure each member of the team takes a turn.

Variation:
Put different vocabulary words or pronouns or numbers or verb tenses, etc. in each grid and have the student pronoun it and make a sentence with it.

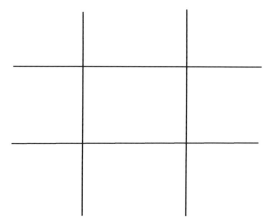

A harder variation:
Place the pictures in the grids upside-down so the students cannot see them before they select one.

Conversation 4

Information questions:

* What is your phone number?
* And what is your address?
* Do you have a business card?

0, 1, 2, 3, 4, 5, 6, 7, 8, 9, 10, 11, 12, 13, 14, 15, 16, 17, 18, 19, 20

21, 22, 23, 24, 25, 26, 27, 28, 29, 30

30, 40, 50, 60, 70, 80 90, 100

* Students practice saying the numbers many times. Then play Ball/Beanbag Toss where the students toss a ball (or anything) back and forth saying the numbers in order as they toss the ball. Intermediate students usually know the numbers, but they need practice pronouncing the number words.

Bean Bag/Ball Toss

This activity can be used with the entire class or in small groups or pairs to practice numbers, vocabulary and the correct sequence of words in proverbs or any sentence.

* Teacher begins by holding the bean bag and saying the first word of the activity.
* Teacher throws the bean bag to a student who says the second word of the activity.
* Student throws the bean bag to any other student who says the next word.
* Continue until the students have said all the words they need to practice.

Example for practicing numbers:
* Teacher begins by holding the bean bag and saying, "One."
* Teacher throws the bean bag to a student who says, "Two."
* Student throws the bean bag to any other student who says, "Three."
* Continue this until the students say all the numbers you wish to practice.
* Alternatives: Start with 10 and count by 10s or count from 11-20.

Objectives

Students will be able to:
1. give basic directions to their residence.
2. read time and date on an appointment card.
3. ask for and show understanding or simple oral directions.
4. read to locate information, places, or directions using a simple map.
5. Identify the 50 US states and capitols through the study of maps.
6. locate places on world, country, and local maps.
7. show understanding of months, days, and seasons.
8. tell time correctly.
9. pronounce ordinal numbers.

Materials Needed for Lesson 3

1. Paper and pens
2. Sign-in sheet for attendence
2. Pictures to illustrate all of the vocabulary
3. Pronunciation and Rhythm charts
4. Song chart - from Lesson 1
5. Name tags for students and teachers
6. 2 flyswatters
7. Maps - world, country, and local
8. Go Fish cards
9. Calendars, clocks, a watch

3 The World

The Beginning of Sin

Theme Picture
Instructions in Lesson 1
Review phone # & address

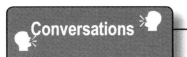

Part 1

Conversation 1

Use a map for this conversation.

* Where are you from? (continent/country)
* What city/town/village?
* Would you show me on the world/country map?
* Tell me about it.
* Tell me about the climate.
* Tell me about the seasons.
* What's the population?
* Are there any unusual sites?

 Have students write about their country and then read it aloud.

Maps

Maps can be used for many teaching points such as directions, prepositions, and geographical terms. Use Total Physical Response (TPR) for much of this lesson. Have students "point to" many things on the world and country maps that are appropriate for your class.

1. Teach the continents. Point to a country and have students name the continent. Teach the English pronunciation for important countries.
2. Allow students plenty of time to talk about their country and what it is like. Use the vocabulary words as you discuss the maps.
3. Use country and local maps to discuss where each person lives and their address.
4. Use prepositions as you discuss where the students are from and where they live.
5. Locate the state and city where you are currently located.

Review addresses many times and many sessions if they need practice <u>saying</u> it.

Conversation 2

A.   Where do you live?
B.   I live at <u>(address)</u> .
A.   Where's that?
B.   It's <u>near</u>_____. *(next to, north of the river)*

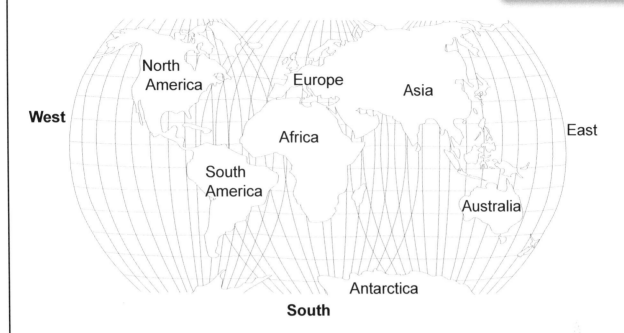

North

North
America

Europe

Asia

West

Africa

East

South
America

Australia

Antarctica

South

Geography words:

continent(s)
country (countries)
state(s)
province(s)
county (counties)
city (cities)
town(s)
village(s)

rural
urban
suburbs
metro

flat
hilly (foothills)
valley(s)
mountain(s)
forest(s)
river(s)
tropical
desert
farmland

Review ordinal numbers from Lesson 1.
Use these prepositions as you discuss the maps.
   I live <u>in</u> North America.   I live <u>next to</u> a river.
   I live <u>on</u> the continent of Asia.   I am <u>from</u> the USA.
   I live <u>near</u> a city.

Song: "He's Got the Whole World in His Hands
    For this lesson put in the names of the continents
    and individual countries.
example:
He's got <u>North America</u> and <u>South America</u> in His hands.
He's got <u>China</u> and <u>Nigeria</u> in His hands.

 **Pronunciation**

Part 1

v	**th** (unvoiced)	**e** (short)
valley	**th**ree	h**ea**vens
village	**th**ird	sp**e**cial
ri**v**er	**th**irteen	pl**ea**sure
hea**v**ens	**th**irty	addr**e**ss
pro**v**ince	four**th**	contin**e**nts
*E**v**e	fif**th**	m**e**tro
*De**v**il	ear**th**	for**e**st
*e**v**il	nor**th**	d**e**sert
*con**v**inced	sou**th**	*D**e**vil
*co**v**ered		*d**e**stroy
*lea**v**e		*s**e**parated

g (hard)	**c** (k)	**a** (long)
be**g**inning	**c**ontinent	teen**a**ger
God	**c**ountry	cre**a**ted
got	**c**arefully	pl**a**ced
girlfriend	**c**alled	m**a**jor
collea**g**ue	**c**ousin	gre**a**t
gorgeous	un**c**le	fian**c**é
***g**arden	un**c**onscious	h**e**y
***g**ood	***c**onvinced	*S**a**tan
***g**ave	***c**overed	*ash**a**med
	***c**rush	***a**te

 The asterisk indicates the words in Part 2.

province
rural
urban
suburb
metro
hilly
foothills
*****know**ledge
*****pun**ished
*****cov**ered
*****E**den

continents
teenager
tropical
provinces
company
Africa
carefully
*****an**imal

Sep**tem**ber
Oc**to**ber
No**vem**ber
De**cem**ber
be**gin**ning
cre**at**ed
fi**an**ceé
to**mor**row
un**con**scious

IDIOMS:

● ●
I'll pick you up.
* I will come and get you.
I'll <u>pick you up</u> at 8:00.

● ● ●   ●
The early bird catches the worm.
* If you are first, you will have more opportunities.
I want to get there early, because <u>the early bird catches the worm</u>.

●   ●
Kick the bucket.
* to die
He <u>kicked the bucket</u>.

Flyswatter Game

After thoroughly teaching the vocabulary, and Prounuciation and Rhythm, make a large chart or write on a board any of the vocabulary words that you want the students to say. Two students are given flyswatters (or anything that can be used to swat) to compete with each other in the game.

The teacher calls out a word and both students "swat" the word. The first to cover the word is the winner. Both students must say the word that is swatted.   A new challenger is then chosen and the game continues. This can also be played in teams with a student from each team competing. The winner gets a point for their team. You can play as long as you like or the first team to get a predetermined number of points wins.

Bible Story

Part 1

The Beginning of Sin

Adam and Eve were happy taking care of the garden. One day Satan, the Devil, talked to Eve. Satan lied and said, "You will not die. You will know all things like God. You will know good and evil". He convinced Eve to eat the fruit from the tree of knowledge of good and evil. She gave some to Adam and he also ate it. They did not obey God. They sinned.

Definitions:

Satan- the Devil
lied - past tense of *lie*, to tell something that is false, untrue
    Discuss when someone has lied to you. What happened?
will not die- future tense, negative; Review death-life from Lesson 2.
know all things - understand everything;
    Can anyone know all things? No, that is a lie.
know good & evil - have a conscience, know right from wrong;
    Discuss right and wrong.
convinced - past tense of *convince*, to talk you into believing;
    Try to talk some one into buying something.
gave - past tense of *give*, handed to; Give someone something and say, "I
    gave Maria a ___." Then have students give examples.
obey - to do what someone tells you to do; Give commands to students and
    when they do it, say "Obey."

Discussion:
1. What was life like for Adam and Eve when they
            were first created?
2. What happened one day?
3. How did the Devil tempt Eve?
4. What did Satan tell Eve?
5. What do you think convinced Eve to eat the fruit?
6. What caused Adam to eat the fruit?
7. What is the cause of sin?

Discuss the lust of the flesh, lust of the eyes, and the pride of life. These are the basis for all sin. Satan still does this today.

Act out as many of the words and concepts as you can rather than merely talk about them.

Part 2

Adam and Eve felt ashamed and hid from God. When God found them, He punished Satan. God said, "The child of a woman will crush you. The Deliverer will destroy you. He told Eve, "You will hurt when you have children." God told Adam, "You will have to work hard to grow food." God killed an animal and covered them with its skin.

God made Adam and Eve leave the Garden of Eden. They were separated from God and began to die.

Taken from Genesis 3

felt - past tense of *feel*, having to do with emotions; Ask how did you feel when ___?" Answer, "I felt ___."

ashamed - past tense of *ashame*, a feeling of guilt: "I felt ashamed when I ___."

hid - to get out of sight; Hide something and say, "I hid the ___."

punished - past tense of *punish*, to cause to suffer for something you did wrong Discuss various forms of punishments.

will crush - future tense, to be totally defeated, to die; Liken this to people getting crushed and killed by falling buildings in an earthquake.

hurt - to have pain; Discuss child birth.

separated - to divide, to split apart; Tear a piece of paper in half and put the pieces far apart and say, "separated."

die - to cease to live, to be separated from God; Review *life-death* from Part 1.

Discussion:
1. What was the first result of their disobedience?
2. What punishment did each one receive?
3. Why is separation from God so bad?
4. Who did God promise to send some day that would destroy Satan?
5. Who do you think is the Deliverer?
6. What did God do to cover Adam and Eve's sin?
7. What was the final punishment?
8. Why is it bad to be separated from God?

Discuss the idea that the sacrifice of blood was necessary to pay for sin and disobedience.

 Close each session with prayer when appropriate. Ask for any prayer requests that your students have.

Conversations

Part 2

Time
hours: minutes
12 : 15

Review time:
There are several ways to tell the time.
3:00 (three o'clock)
1:05 (one 0 five) five minutes after 1
2:30 (two thirty) half past 2
3: 15 (three fifteen) quarter past 3
4:45 (four forty-five) quarter to 5
15:30 (fifteen hundred hours and 30 minutes)
    military/international time
a.m.- after midnight   p.m. - afternoon

* hour: minutes, o'clock, minutes after, half past, quarter past, quarter to, am - pm

Conversation 1

A. Excuse me, what time is it?
      (*What time do you have?*)
      (*What time is it, please?*)
B. It's 12:15.
A. Thank you very much.
B. You're welcome.

Polite Expressions:
please
thank you
thank you very much
excuse me
you're welcome

Conversation 2

When are you meeting _____?
When is your appointment?

Discuss appointments:
* doctor, dentist, etc.
* personal (meeting for lunch)
* business (meeting a client)
* church meetings
* pleasure (movies, concerts)
* class meetings

Use a calendar to review these words.

REVIEW

Time -	Seasons -	Days -	Months-	
year	Winter	Sunday (Sun.)	January	July
today	Spring	Monday (Mon,)	February	August
yesterday	Summer	Tuesday (Tues.)	March	September
tomorrow	Fall (Autumn)	Wednesday (Wed.)	April	October
morning		Thursday (Thurs.)	May	November
afternoon		Friday (Fri.)	June	December
evening		Saturday (Sat.)		

In America we write the date:
month, day, year.
Other countries write:
day, month, year.

Numbers:
* review numbers 0 - 59 for telling time

Play the **NUMBER GAME.**
Use a deck of number cards (UNO) or write numbers 0-9 on index cards. Make 5 sets. Shuffle the cards and hand one to each player face up. Ask each student to say the number on their card. Then hand out a second card. Students can put the second number in front or behind the first card and say the 2-digit number. Hand out a third card and the student says the 4-digit number. Continue playing as long as there are cards left in the deck.

Activities

Part 2

 Use the "Line Up" game to practice
ordinal numbers

Ordinal numbers:
first
second
third
fourth
fifth
sixth
seventh
eighth
ninth
tenth

Prepositions:
in, on, near,
closer, closest
next to, from,
front, back,
front of the line
end of the line
middle, between

Directions:
left
right

Idiom

Ticks me off
*really makes me mad
He is always saying bad things about me. He really <u>ticks me off</u>.

Line Up

The **Line Up** is a good activity for teaching directions, prepositions and numbers, including ordinal numbers (first, second, third, etc.) The basic **Line Up** might help beginners with the **Hokey Pokey** or **Simon Says**.

Basic Line Up for directions:
* Line the students up side by side.
* The tutor asks questions and gives commands.
    * Where are your hands?
    * Where is your left hand? (Show them if they do not know.)
    * Where is your right hand? (Again, show them if they do not know.)
    * Who is on your right? (Listen to each student tell who is on his right?)
    * Who is on your left? (Again, listen to each student.)
    * Turn left. (Demonstrate turning 1/4 turn.)
    * Turn right. (Demonstrate any commands if necessary.)
    * Walk straight ahead.
    * Stop.
    * Do any variation of the above commands for more practice. Add new ones.

Line Up for reviewing or teaching prepositions and close/far/closer/closest:
* Line the students up side by side.
* The tutor asks questions and gives commands. Some examples are:
    * Who is next to you? (Listen to each student's answer to each question.)
    * Who is beside you?
    * Who is far from you?
    * Who is closer to you, _____ or _____. Who is closest?
    * Who is closer to you? (Have each student make their own sentence.)
    * Who is between ___ and ___.

Line Up for cardinal numbers (1, 2, 3, 4...):
* Line the students up front to back, one at a time, by giving these commands:
    * Mary, please come here. You are Student #1.
    * David, you are Student #2.
    * Continue until all students are in line.
    * Ask what number each student is. They say: I am # ___.
    * Each student says what number the other students are: Mary is #1, etc.

Line Up for ordinal numbers (1st, 2nd, 3rd, 4th...) and behind/in front of:
* Line the students up front to back, using ordinal numbers (first, second, third, etc.):
    * Each student says which place he is in line: I am first, etc.
    * Move the 1st student to the end. Ask the students what place they are in.
    * Mix the students up and ask what place they are in again.
* Teach behind & in front of in a similar manner.

Objectives

Students will be able to:

1. Interpret and show understanding of basic weather safety warnings.
2. Show understanding of weather terms and names of common animals.
3. Demonstrate knowledge of weather related clothing.
4. Understand what to do in weather emergencies.
5. Increase vocabulary of animal names.

Materials Needed for Lesson 4

1. Paper and pens (Sign In chart)
2. Pictures to illustrate all of the vocabulary
   (Use a Picture Dictionary)
3. Pronunciation and Rhythm charts
4. Song chart - "Old Noah had a Boat"
   (Tune - Old McDonald)
5. Name tags for students and teachers

4 Weather & Animals

The Flood

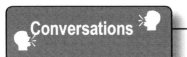
Conversations

Part 1

 Get pictures from your local weather office or the internet.

1. Discussion questions about weather:
    What will the weather be like today?
    What is the forecast?
    What's the weather like outside?
    What should I wear?
    What's the temperature?
2. Discuss different types of weather.
    Talk about the different types of weather in different
        seasons in your area.
    Compare & contrast it to student's native country.
    Talk about preparations to make for each kind.
    What should you wear when it's ___?
    Talk about storms and safety (especially for your area).

Summer

Spring

Winter

Autumn
- Fall

WEATHER:

forecast
sunny
rainy, misty
foggy
cloudy, partly
snowy, icy
hot
cold
mild
windy
stormy
rainbow
drenched
sleet
hail

STORMS:

tornado
hurricane
thunder storm
typhoon
snow storm
blizzard
ice storm
rainy season
dry season
flood

CLOTHES:

a coat
a raincoat
an umbrella
a sweater
gloves
a scarf
boots
a hoodie
a sweatshirt
snow shoes

temperature
Fahrenheit - F
Celsius - C
degrees - 75°

IDIOMS:

● ●
under the weather.
*sick
I have had the flu.
I've been <u>under the weather</u>.

● ●
When it rains it pours.
* when something bad
happens, several more
bad things happen.

My car broke down. My dog died.
Then I got sick. <u>When it rains it pours</u>.

● ● ●
Raining cats and dogs.
*raining a lot
It's really coming down.
It's <u>raining cats and dogs</u>.

● ● ●
Clouds with a silver lining
* Even though you have trouble, something good can come out of it.
While getting my car fixed, I met a really nice girl. That <u>cloud had a silver lining.</u>

 **Pronunciation**

Part 1

p	**t**	**o** (long)	**oo**
partly	**t**emperture	**o**kay	m**oo**n
pre**p**arations	**t**oday	**o**bey	t**o**day
population	**t**ypes	sn**ow**	aftern**oo**n
province	**t**ornado	rainb**ow**	typh**oo**n
punished	**t**ropical	c**o**ld	*z**oo**
***p**et	**t**otally	rainc**o**at	*t**o**
***p**ig	**t**omorrow	tornad**o**	*t**oo**
***p**arrot	***t**iger	*N**o**ah	*tw**o**
*a**pp**eared		*buffal**o**	
***p**romised		*g**o**at	

sh	**k**	**s** (end-z)	**i** (short)
shines	**k**ind	preparation**s**	m**i**sty
shirt	**k**id	storm**s**	w**i**ndy
should	ma**k**e	tornadoe**s**	bl**i**zzard
fre**sh**man	o**k**ay	hurricane**s**	s**i**lver
sweat**sh**irt	wor**k**ing	typhoon**s**	trop**i**cal
*wor**sh**ip	li**k**e	blizzard**s**	d**i**scuss
*fini**sh**ed	*clo**ck**	*season**s**	d**i**fferent
*puni**sh**	***k**ill	*dog**s**	*pr**i**vilege
*a**sh**amed	*mon**k**ey	*rain**s**	*b**ui**ld
***sh**eep	*chi**ck**en	*pour**s**	*an**i**mals
	*don**k**ey	*shine**s**	*del**i**vered

 *The asterisks indicate the words for Part 2

Proverb

● ● ● ●

The sun shines on the good and the bad.
* good things happen to good and bad people

56

thunder storm
dry season
hurricane
*__vi__olent
*__dif__ferent
*__priv__ilege
*__to__tally
*__af__ternoon
*__buf__falo
*__el__ephant

Aus**tral**ia
um**brel**la
tor**na**do
a **hood**ie
a **sweat**er
*a **sweat**shirt
*a **rain**coat
*to**mor**row

weather
forecast
ice storm
silver
lining
foggy
icy
*__rab__bit
*__cam__el
*__li__on
*__ang__ry

Song: **Old Man Noah had a Boat**
tune - Old McDonald had a Farm

Verse:
Old man Noah had a boat,
E-I-E-I-O
And on this boat he had 2 <u>animals</u>,
E-I-E-I-O
With a <u>animal sound</u> here,
And a <u>animal sound</u> there.
Here a <u>animal sound</u>.
There a <u>animal sound.</u>
Everywhere a <u>animal sound</u>.
Old man Noah had a boat.
E-I-E-I-O

Continue putting different animals in the song.
Sing as many times as you like.

Part 1

The Flood

Many people were born, but God became angry with the people on earth because they were cruel and violent. All of the people were very evil, except Noah and his family. Noah and his family worshiped and obeyed God.

So God told Noah, "Build a big boat. Put your family and many of the animals in the boat because I am going to send a flood and destroy everything." Noah obeyed God and built the boat. When the boat was finished Noah and his family and the animals went into it. God closed the door of the boat.

Definitions:

angry - mad, rage, wrath; Stomp around the room and say,"I'm angry!" Discuss what makes you feel angry.
because - the reason for something
cruel - mean, causing injury & pain
violent - bad actions; fighting and killing
Discuss things that are cruel and violent.
except - not
worshiped - praise and singing, deep respect or honor
build - make, construct; Show picture from charts.
flood - to cover with water; Show picture from charts.
destroy - to put to an end, do away with
everything - all things
finished - past tense of *finish*, complete; Show pictures
closed - past tense of *close*, shut

Discussion questions:

1. What happened after Adam and Eve sinned?
2. How did God feel about people?
3. What were the people like?
4. Finally, who were the only people who worshiped and obeyed God?
5. What did God tell Noah to do?
6. What was God going to do?
7. Did Noah obey God? Why?
7. What did Noah and his family do when the boat was finished?
8. Who closed the door?

 Close each session with prayer when appropriate. Ask for any prayer requests that your students have.

Act out and discuss as many of the words and concepts as you can rather than merely talk about them. Use the words in sentences and have the students make up sentences as well. Show pictures from the charts.

Part 2

It rained for forty days and nights and everything was covered with water for 150 days. Finally the water started to go down and the ground appeared again. Then Noah, his family, and the animals came out of the boat. God delivered them from the flood.

They worshiped God, and God promised that a flood of water would never cover the whole earth again. The rainbow is a sign of that promise.

Genesis 6-8

Definitions:

covered - past tense of *cover,* spread over

started - past tense of *start,* begin; Opposites start-finish

appeared - past tense of *appear.* to see, made visible

delivered - past tense of *deliver,* saved

promised - past tense of *promise,* keep your word. do as you say

rainbow - an arc or circle of colors that is formed by the refraction of sunrays through raindrops

sign - something you can see

Discussion questions:

1. How long did it rain?
2. How long did water cover the earth?
3. What had God done for Noah and the animals?
3. What did Noah and his family do when they got off the boat?
4. What did God promise?
5. What is a sign of that promise?
6. Should God punish sin?
7. What did Noah do that made him different from other people?
8. How can we obey God?

Jesus mentions the Flood in Matthew 16:2&3

Part 2

Discuss animals:
Do you have a pet?
    What kind of pet? Describe.
    Where did you get it?
    How long have you had it?
Have you ever been to the zoo?
    What did you see?
    What kind of animals do you like / dislike?
Have you ever been fishing / hunting?
    What animals did you catch? Kill?
Have you ever lived on a farm?
    What kind of animals live on a farm?
    Tell about farm animals in your local area.
    Tell about farm animals in your native country.
    Compare & contrast farms.
What are tame and wild animals?
Name the ones of interest to you.

PETS:
a dog
a cat
a bird
a horse
a fish

FARM ANIMALS:
a cow
a horse
a goat
a sheep
a rabbit
a pig
a donkey
a water buffalo
a chicken
a duck

Use many pictures from books, magazines, calendars, etc. to teach the names of the animals

If your city has a zoo, you may want to take a field trip as a class. This is a perfect activity to do for this lesson.

ZOO ANIMALS:
a giraffe
a monkey
an elephant
a zebra
a panda
a lion
a tiger
an ostrich
a polar bear
a parrot

Objectives

Students will be able to:

1. Ask for and show understanding of simple oral directions.
2. Ask for clarification of directions.
3. Ask for common community services such as library card or school enrollment.
4. Recognize, read, and write money related symbols.
5. Read to locate information using simple schedules.
6. Understand US money and its value and apply this knowledge to basic personal needs.
7. Open a checking or savings account.
8. Identify key places in their community and access their services.
9. Know and/or be able to ask for the basic information and services from each of the key places in their community.

Materials Needed for Lesson 5

1. Paper and pens (Sign In chart)
2. Pictures to illustrate all of the vocabulary
3. Pronunciation and Rhythm charts
4. Song chart - "Father Abraham"
5. Name tags for students and teachers
6. Local maps
7. Large charts for drawing maps
8. Markers to draw maps
9 Small toy vehicles to move on the drawn maps as you give directions

5　Getting to Travel

The Promise through Abraham

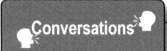
Conversations

Part 1

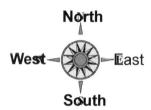
North

West — — East

South

a map

Direction Discussions:

Excuse me, How do I get to ___?
   (Start in the northwest corner to give directions.)
            * the Center
            * the post Office
            * the bus Station
            * the train Station
            * the school
            * the market
            * the coffee shop
            * etc.
* Model by asking your partner or one of the students to give you
   directions using this map. Practice using the vocabulary
   words as you give directions to each other.   In Session 2 use
   a local map.
   Then have students ask each other until they feel comfortable
   telling another person how to get to a certain place.
* To ask directions to the bathroom, start with the building in
   which you are having your class. Discuss the different names
   for "Restroom" in your location.
* Then do the activity on the following pages to practice giving
   and following directions more.

a map

Directions:

straight ahead

left   right

on the left   on the right
turn left   turn right

The Center
North

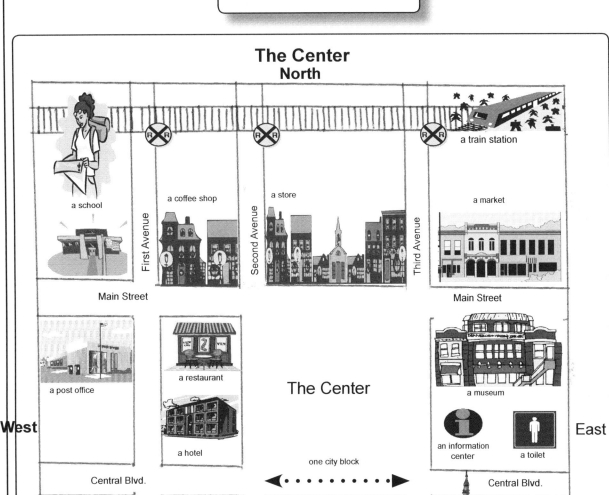

a train station

a school

a coffee shop

a store

a market

First Avenue

Second Avenue

Third Avenue

Main Street

Main Street

a post office

a restaurant

The Center

a museum

West

East

a hotel

an information center

a toilet

Central Blvd.

one city block

Central Blvd.

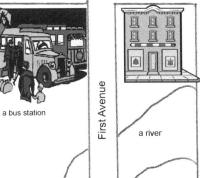

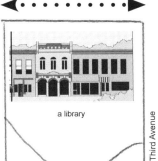

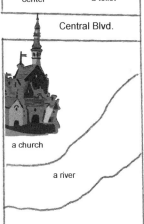

a bus station

First Avenue

a river

Second Avenue

a library

Third Avenue

a church

a river

a river

South

Choose one of these 2 activities to do with your class.

Map (Personal Map)

* Give each student a piece of paper.
* Ask them to draw a small picture of their house (apartment, flat) in the center.
* Model this as you go by drawing your own on either a chalk or white board or a
     large sheet of paper so all can see.
* After you model that, say, "I live **in** a house" or whatever kind of structure you live in.
* Each student should then personalize their statement about their living
     arrangements.
* Continue modeling the following things, with students personalizing them:
     #1--Draw the street you live **on** and name it. I live **on** ___.
     #2--Draw something **next to/near/across from** your house, saying _____
          is **next to (near, across from)** my house (apartment, flat).
     #3--Draw your neighborhood/city/state or province/country and continent,
          naming each one as you go.
* Make a complete sentence with each one. For example, I live **in** New York City.

* Be sure to have your students **say** what they are drawing. You may want them to
     pair up or work in small groups for this activity. Your job as teacher will be to
     encourage them to speak! The purpose of this activity is to have the students
     using the appropriate prepositions in as many instances as possible.

Part 1

Map (Interactive Map)

Interactive maps are excellent ways to teach prepositions, directions and community vocabulary.

Pre-class preparations:
* Gather materials: large butcher/chart paper, pencils, erasers, and markers/crayons plus toy cars or similar objects, such as a pack of gum, to use as vehicles.
* Tutors draw several basic maps on large chart paper, one map per 4 students.
* Draw 3 streets going vertically and 3 horizontally with a river cutting across several streets so there are bridges to cross. Include a railroad track as well.
* Draw a well-known building somewhere on the maps, such as a museum.

* In class, teaching prepositions:
* Divide the class into groups of about 4 per map.
*Tell the 1st student in each group to draw a church (or any vocabulary word) next to the museum, or the building you drew.
* Have different students draw various buildings in response to these instructions:

    Draw _____ near the _____.
    Draw _____beside the _____.
    Draw _____across from the _____.
    Draw _____ on 1st Street (Main Street, New York Ave, Paris Circle)
    Draw a parking lot next to _____.
    Draw a car in the parking lot.

* Draw as much as time allows, using the maps for discussions about the community, as well as learning the prepositions.

In class, teaching directions:
* Use toy cars to role-play the conversations and expand them.
* Have a student drive as you instruct them: Drive straight ahead, turn left, etc.
* Demonstrate where to drive the vehicle using the conversations in the following group and paired activities.

Group activity:
 Ask your partner or a student the first question: Excuse me, where's the bus station? Have them give you the directions. Drive your toy car according to those directions, such as straight ahead, turn to the left and turn to the right, as he gives the directions and say the direction sentences as you go. Repeat this exercise with every student, having them drive to different places. If the class is larger than 6, divide into groups for this activity. Have a helper facilitating each group.

Paired activity:
Have students give and follow each other's directions in pairs. Be sure to have the student following the directions (driving the car) as they are being given.

.

 **Pronunciation**

Part 1

soft c
city
center
central
office
except
*police
*descendant
*ancestor
*certain

soft g
package
message
teenager
knowledge
*village
*giraffe
*privilege
*generation
*Egypt

s (z)
hands
closed
days
causing
because
actions
*visible
*animals
*farms
*Israel

long u
usual
usually
beautiful
you
nephew
*university
*population

x
exit
excuse
next
*exclude
*except
*experience

hard c
country
cost
account
come
Canaan
because
*curse
*become
*completely
*Isaac
*conversation

hard g
going
getting
give
together
*God
*good
*again
*organization

short o
God
office
coffee
shop
block
*honor
*promise
*October
*sophomore
*tropical
*population

*The asterisks indicate the words for Part 2

visible
privilege
straight ahead
avenue
*****A**braham
*****fam**ily
*****fi**nally
*****an**cestor
*****Is**rael

Ex**cuse** me
You're **wel**come
the **Cen**ter
some **ice** cream
in **front** of
di**rec**tions
*****com**plete**ly
*****to**geth**er
*****Mess**i**ah
*****de**scend**ants

the **post** office
the **bus** station
the **train** station
a **bus** ticket
the **coffee** shop
the **lib**rary
a **rest**aurant
*****De**liv**erer

IDIOMS:

●
In the red
*You have more debt than money.
I have too much debt.
I am <u>in the red</u>.

● ●
Hit the road
*leave, go away
I told him to <u>hit the road</u>.

●
In the black
*You have more money than debts.
I have money in my bank account.
I am <u>in the black</u>.

●
Let's roll.
*let's go
We are going on a trip.
<u>Let's roll.</u>

● ● ● ●
Throw someone under the bus.
*to let someone else get the blame
When the company failed, he <u>threw the employees under the bus.</u>

69

Bible Story

Act out and discuss as many of the words and concepts as you can rather than merely talk about them. Use the words in sentences and have the students make up sentences as well. Show pictures from the charts.

Part 1

Travel

Many generations after Noah, there was a man named Abraham. God said to Abraham, "Leave your country and move to a land that I will show you. I will be with you, and your family will become a great nation. You will be famous and all nations will be blessed because you honor Me. I will bless anyone who blesses you and will curse anyone who curses you. Your family will go to Egypt to live for 400 years, and become slaves. Then I will bring them back to this land and give it to them."

Definitions:

Generations - discuss descendants and ancestors
   ancestors - the people born <u>before</u> you in your family
   descendants - the people born <u>after</u> you in your family
Canaan / Israel - a small country in the Middle East
nation - a country and a political group of people
bless - to say and do something good for someone
curse - to say and do something bad to someone
Egypt - a country in northeast Africa
slaves - people who are owned by other people

Discussion Questions:
1. Who was born many generations later?
2. What did God tell Abraham to do?
3. What did God promise Abraham?
4. What great nation did Abraham's family become?
5. Is Abraham famous? Why?
6. Are all nations blessed because of Abraham? How?
7. What happens to those who bless the Jews?
8. What happens to those who curse the Jews?
9. What was going to happen to Abraham's family for 400 years?
10. Then what would happen?

Part 2

One of your family members will obey Me completely and bring people and God together again." He will be the Deliverer. Abraham believed what God told him.

When Abraham and his wife Sarah were very old they had a baby boy named Isaac. Everything God told Abraham came true.   It was through him God blessed the whole world by sending the Deliverer.

Genesis 12-50

Definitions:
believe - to think in a certain way based on facts and experiences
chosen - picked out of a group
Deliverer - the one who was to come and bring God and man together again

Discussion Questions:
1. What was one special person in
   Abraham's family going to do?
2. Who was that person?
3. Did Abraham believe God?
4. What did God do for Sarah?
5. Who is the promised family?
6. Did the promises come true?
7. How did God bless the whole world?
8. How are we blessed today?

 Close each session with prayer when appropriate. Ask for any prayer requests that your students have.

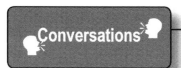

Conversations

Part 2

a train station

a bus station

a post office

a coffee shop/
a restaurant

a museum

Conversations:
* at the post office
  I need to mail __. I need to buy some stamps.
  Mailing letters, packages, money orders
* at the police station
  report a crime
* at the bus / train station
  I need a ticket to ____. (a city, country)
  Talk about bus/train schedules
* at a coffee shop/ restaurant
  I would like to order ___.
* at a hotel
  I need a room for __ night(s).
* at a school
  I am here to enroll my child.
* at a church
  I would like to talk to the pastor / priest.
* at a museum
  How much does a ticket cost?
* at the market / grocery store
  I would like to buy ___. How much does it cost?
* at the library
  How do I check out a book?
* at the bank
  I would like to open an account.

a hotel

a school

a market/grocery store

a church

a toilet
a restroom
WC

ATM

Phone conversations:

* Hi, I'm going to ___ .
  Can you meet me there at ___?
  Sure, how do I get there?
  Where is it?

* Hi, Jim and I are meeting Alice
  later at ___.
  Would you like to come?
  Yes, how do I get there?
  Where is it?
  What time are you meeting?

* Hi, I'm / we're going to ___.
  Would you like to come?
  Sure, where is it?
  How do I get there?

Money
*Talk about different
currencies.

American currency:
   dollars/cents
   quarters
   dimes
   nickels
   pennies

 **Pronunciation**

Part 2

soft c
city
center
central
office
except
*police
*descendant
*ancestor
*certain

soft g
package
message
teenager
knowledge
*village
*giraffe
*privilege
*generation
*Egypt

s (z)
hands
closed
days
causing
because
actions
*visible
*animals
*farms
*Israel

long u
usual
usually
beautiful
you
nephew
*university
*population

x
exit
excuse
next
*exclude
*except
*experience

hard c
country
cost
account
come
Canaan
because
*curse
*become
*completely
*Isaac
*conversation

hard g
going
getting
give
together
*God
*good
*again
*organization

short o
God
office
coffee
shop
block
*honor
*promise
*October
*sophomore
*tropical
*population

● ● **●** ●

information
gener**a**tion
at the st**a**tion
popul**a**tion
a great **na**tion
special **mem**ber

● **●** ●

Ex**cuse** me
You're **wel**come
the **Cen**ter
some **ice** cream
in **front** of
dir**ec**tions

● ● ●

post office
bus station
train station
bus ticket
straight ahead
library

IDIOMS: Review

Money talks
* to bribe someone

Kick up your heels
* to go out and party

For a song
* to buy something for very little money

In the hole
* to have a lot of debt

 **Activities**

Part 2

ஃ Map (Interactive Map)

Use the same maps that you drew in the last session to practice more.

In class, teaching directions:
* Use toy cars to role-play the conversations and expand them.
* Have a student drive as you instruct them: Drive straight ahead, turn left, etc.
* Demonstrate where to drive the vehicle using the conversations in the following group and paired activities.

Group activity:
 Ask your partner or a student the first question: Excuse me, where's the bus station? Have them give you the directions. Drive your toy car according to those directions, such as straight ahead, turn to the left and turn to the right, as he gives the directions and say the direction sentences as you go. Repeat this exercise with every student, having them drive to different places. If the class is larger than 6, divide into groups for this activity. Have a helper facilitating each group.

Paired activity:
Have students give and follow each other's directions in pairs. Be sure to have the student following the directions (driving the car) as they are being given.
.

ஃ Song: "Father Abraham"

Father Abraham had many sons,
Many sons had Father Abraham,
And I am one of them and so are you,
So let's just praise the Lord,
Right arm, (move your right arm back and forth)

Repeat verse while moving your right arm.
On the last line of the verse say, "Left arm". (Move both arms as you sing.)

Repeat the verse while moving both arms.
On the last line say,"Right leg". (Move both arms and right leg.)

Repeat the verse while moving both arms and right leg.
On the last leg say, "Left leg". (Move both arms and both legs.)

Repeat verse one more time moving both arms and legs, but on the last line say,"Hallelujah, sit down."

Game "TRAVEL"

First person says, " I am going on a trip and I put a ___ in my suitcase."
Second person says, "   "   "   "   "   "   " a (first person's thing) and a ___ ."
Third person says,   "   "   " a (first person's thing) and a
 (second person's thing) and a ___ ".
Etc. and each person says the things that the others have put in the suitcase and
then adds one more. It keeps going around the circle until the last person has had a
turn. If you only have a few students, go around several times.
The last person says," That is all I can get into my suitcase."
You can give the students guidelines for things to be put into the suitcase such as;
animals, clothes, kitchen items, or just make it random and silly.

OBJECTIVES

Students will be able to:

1. Ask for and give personal information.
2. State need for frequently used materials in the home.
3. Ask about rent or about basic housing needs, and request repairs in simple terms.
4. Recognize the names of household things.

Materials Needed for Lesson 6

1. Paper and pens (Sign In chart)
2. Pictures to illustrate all of the vocabulary
   (a picture dictionary)
3. Pronunciation and Rhythm charts
4. Song chart -
5. Name tags for students and teachers
6. Local maps
7. Large charts for drawing maps
8. Markers to draw maps
9 Small toy vehicles to move on the drawn
   maps as you give directions

6 Homes

Moses

Part 1

Discussion Questions:
(Students work in pairs and ask each other these questions.)

Apartments or Flats
We are looking for (an apartment / flat).
We are looking for (one) bedroom, and (one) bath.
What is available?
How many rooms does it have?
How much is the rent? Deposit?
Does that include utilities?
How much do utilities cost?
When is the rent payment due?
How many months is the contract?
    (Be sure to have somone you trust look over the contract.)
Does it include the ___?(washer & dryer, garage, fireplace)
    (In some places you may ask if they have electricity & water.)
Is there an elevator? or stairs?
Where do you park your car? Is there a parking fee?
Where is the nearest bus stop?
What kind of security do you have?
Do you have cable hookup? dish satelite?
Do you have a laundry room?
What floor is the apartment on?
When can we come and look at the apartment?

Houses or Mobile Homes
What's the asking price? (house / mobile home)
How many bedrooms and bathrooms does it have?
How many square feet of living space are in the house?
How much do utilities run?
How much are the taxes?
How much is the insurance?
Does it include the ___?
    (washer & dryer, fireplace, refrigerator, stove)
How old is the house?
    (roof, appliances, air conditioner, heater, hot water heater)

 Use a picture dictionary or
magazine pictures to show
the vocabulary.

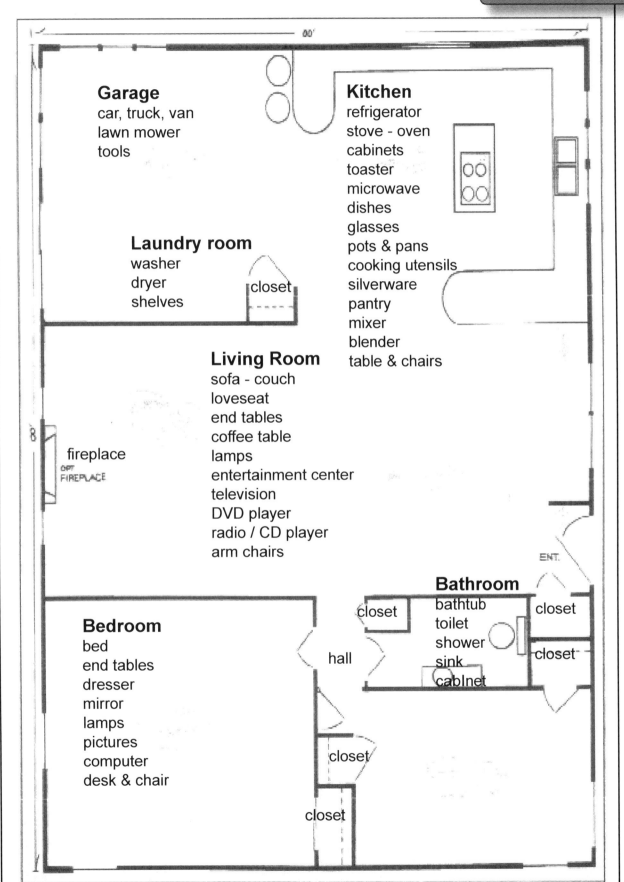

Garage
car, truck, van
lawn mower
tools

Kitchen
refrigerator
stove - oven
cabinets
toaster
microwave
dishes
glasses
pots & pans
cooking utensils
silverware
pantry
mixer
blender
table & chairs

Laundry room
washer
dryer
shelves

closet

Living Room
sofa - couch
loveseat
end tables
coffee table
lamps
entertainment center
television
DVD player
radio / CD player
arm chairs

fireplace

OPT
FIREPLACE

Bathroom
bathtub
toilet
shower
sink
cabinet

closet

closet

closet

ENT.

hall

Bedroom
bed
end tables
dresser
mirror
lamps
pictures
computer
desk & chair

closet

closet

81

 **Pronunciation**

Part 1

y	**-y**	**st**	**-st**
you	man**y**	**st**ove	co**st**
your	securit**y**	**st**ate	ea**st**
you're	laundr**y**	**st**ore	we**st**
young	pantr**y**	**st**ation	re**st**
***y**es	*electricit**y**	***st**ars	*fir**st**
***y**esterday	*balcon**y**	***st**airs	*tru**st**
***y**ear	*completel**y**	***st**op	*neare**st**
	*universit**y**		

or	**-er**	**long i**	**u-oo**
f**or**	wat**er**	satell**i**te	Febr**u**ary
f**or**ty	wash**er**	f**i**replace	J**u**ne
flo**or**	dry**er**	m**i**crowave	J**u**ly
do**or**	mow**er**	dry**er**	T**u**esday
sophom**or**e	heat**er**	dr**i**ve	cr**u**el
b**or**n	mix**er**	*d**i**ning	tr**ue**
***or**der	*cent**er**	*gu**i**de	*thro**u**gh
*rep**or**t	*play**er**	*Israel**i**te	*r**u**lers
*n**or**th	*show**er**	*N**i**le	*incl**u**de
*c**or**ner	*dress**er**	*l**i**fe	*d**ue**
*b**or**der	*riv**er**		*comp**u**ter

*The asterisks indicate the words for Part 2

● **●** ●

apartment
deposit
a **kit**chen
a **bed**room
a **bath**room
a **clos**et
*a **base**ment
*a **stair**way
*a **con**tract
*com**plete**ly
*in**sur**ance

● ● **●** ● ●

the u**til**ities
the se**cur**ity
*elec**tric**ity
*uni**ver**sity

● ● ●

living room
dining room
balcony
patio
parking fee

IDIOMS

● **●** ● **●**

Get up on the wrong side of the bed
* to act in a grouchy manner
He is so grouchy. He must <u>have gotten up</u>
<u>on the wrong side of the bed.</u>

● ●

Hit the sack
*Go to bed
I am tired. I think
I will <u>hit the sack.</u>

● ● ● ●

Drive someone up a wall
* Drive someone crazy
She <u>drives me up the wall</u>.

● ● ●

Put something on the back burner
* to change plans.
I wanted to buy a new car, but I got sick
so I had to <u>put it on the back burner.</u>

Bible Story

Part 1

Home

Abraham had a son named Isaac. Isaac had a son named Jacob, and God changed Jacob's name to Israel. Israel had 12 sons who became the nation of Israel. They are also called Jews.

Many years after Abraham lived, the Jews moved to Egypt because there was a severe drought. They lived there for a long time. As the pharaohs changed, the Israelites became the slaves of the Egyptians.

One evil pharaoh wanted to kill all of the Jewish baby boys because there were too many Israelites. So a Jewish mother hid her baby boy in a little boat along the bank of the Nile River. God used the daughter of the Egyptian ruler to save the child and let him grow up. She called the baby Moses.

Definitions:
Jews - Israelites
Severe - a lot, extreme, of a great degree
drought - no rain for a long time
pharoah - an Egyptian ruler, a king
Nile River - famous river on the eastern border of
            Egypt
bank - the edge of the river

Jewish home

Discussion Questions:
1. Who was the son of Isaac? Jacob?
2. How many sons did Jacob have?
3. What did they become?
4. What are the Israelites also called?
5. Why did they go to Egypt?
6. What happened after many years?
7. What did one evil pharoah do to limit the number of Israelites?
8. What did one mother do to save her baby?
9. How did God save her baby?

Act out as many of the words and concepts as you can rather than merely talk about them.

Part 2

Moses grew up in the palace. He was educated and became a prince.

One day Moses got angry with an Egyptian who was beating an Israelite. Moses killed the Egyptian and then ran for his life. He went to a desert country called Midian. Moses was no longer a prince. He became a shepherd.

Much later God came and talked to Moses from a burning bush. God said, "Return to Egypt and lead the Israelites out of Egypt. I will be with you and guide you."

Definitions:
palace - home of the Pharoah
educated - had many years of schooling
prince - son of a pharoah
angry - mad
ran for his life - leave the country to avoid being killed
Midian - an area southeast of Egypt (see the map)
shepherd - a person who takes care of sheep
burning bush - The bush was burning, but it didn't burn up.
return - go back
lead - to go in front, be the guide
guide - show someone the best way to go

Discussion Questions:
1. Where did Moses grow up?
2. What happened as he was growing up?
3. What did Moses do one day after he was a grown man?
4. What did Moses do to avoid punishment?
5. Where did he go?
6. What was his job?
7. After many years what did God tell Moses to do?
8. How did He tell Moses?
9. Does God watch over us like He did with Moses?
10. Does God talk to us? How?
11. Does God stay with us and guide us? How?

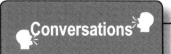 Conversations

Part 2

It's moving day:
Where should we put the ___?
      Please put the ___ in the ___.
      Please put the ___ beside the ___.
      Please put the ___ next to the ___.

Where do you want the ___?
Be careful with the ___. It is fragile.
Where is / are the ___?

Arrange an apartment / house.

1. Give each student a paper. Have them draw a plan of their own home. Then have them draw where things are placed in their home. Have each student describe a room and the things in the room to a partner.

2. Give each person a blank home plan and have them design the rooms placing each item where they think they should go and then tell each other how they would decorate their own home.

THINGS IN THE HOME

Living room
sofa - couch
loveseat
end tables
coffee table
lamps
entertainment center
television
DVD player
radio / CD player
arm chairs

Kitchen
refrigerator
stove - oven
cabinets
toaster
microwave
dishes
glasses
pots & pans
cooking utensils
silverware
pantry
mixer
blender
table & chairs

Bedroom
bed
end tables
dresser
mirror
lamps
pictures
computer
desk & chair

Bathroom
bathtub
toilet
shower
sink
cabinet

Laundry room
washer
dryer
shelves

Garage
car, truck, van
lawn mower
tools

OBJECTIVES

Students will be able to:
1. Recognize the names of foods.
2. Order food at a restaurant.
3. Talk about social etiquette at a restaurant.
4. Recognize, read and reproduce basic symbols and abbreviations used on food labels.
5. Complete basic math computations and read a restaurant or grocery bill.
6. Understand and read food measurements for recipes.

Materials Needed for Lesson 7

1. Paper and pens
2. Pictures to illustrate all of the vocabulary
3. Pronunciation and Rhythm charts
4. Song chart -
5. Name tags for students and teachers
6. Old menus
7. A map of the middle east
8. Several boxes, cans, or jars with labels

7   Food

Passover

Conversations

Part 1

Discussions about food:
Discuss what you would eat for a typical breakfast, lunch, and dinner.
Discuss recipes and the English measurements.
Discuss food preparations & safety.
Discuss healthy eating.

Make up a menu:
(Have students write their menu)
Make a menu for:
   breakfast
   lunch
   dinner
Make a menu for:
   a restaurant
   a party
   a wedding dinner
   a picnic

Use a picture dictionary or magazine pictures to show the vocabulary.

Lunch

Breakfast

coffee / tea
toast, biscuits
eggs
bacon / ham / sauage
cereal / oatmeal
pancakes
fruit juice
milk / yogurt

pop / soda (Coke)
tea
sandwiches
hamburger
french fries
chips
lettuce
tomato
onion
pickle
mayonnaise
mustard
ketchup

Dinner

meat-	chicken, fish, hamburger, lamb, turkey
vegetables-	tomatoes, onions, corn, herbs, lettuce,cabbage, potatoes, beans
fruit-	apples, bananas, pears, grapes, oranges, grapefruit
grains-	rice, wheat, oats, cereal, bread
dairy-	milk, cheese, ice cream, yogurt, butter
spices-	salt, pepper, basil, oregano, parsley, garlic, ginger, curry, sage, cinnamon, chili powder

 **Pronunciation**

Part 1

ch	**l**	**d**	**j**
lun**ch**	**l**unch	**d**inner	**j**uice
sandwi**ch**	**l**amb	**d**ining room	ma**j**or
fren**ch** fries	**l**ettuce	**d**rought	**J**ews
chips	**l**iving room	**d**aughter	**J**ewish
ket**ch**up	**l**ived	**d**egree	***J**esus
chicken	**l**ife	**d**octor	*in**j**ury
***ch**eese	***l**ead	***d**esert	
*kit**ch**en	***l**eave	***d**ied	
*_**ch**urch_	***l**ong	***d**eath	
*cou**ch**	***l**ittle	***d**oorpost	
*_**ch**air_	***l**and		

c (s)	**short o**	**short oo**	**long oo**
cents	**o**nion	t**oo**k	f**oo**d
gro**c**ery	bac**o**n	h**oo**d	m**oo**n
ri**c**e	st**o**mach	h**oo**die	s**oo**n
cereal	c**o**vered	*c**oo**ked	t**oo**
cinnamon	m**o**ney	*l**oo**ked	*z**oo**
*i**c**e	*fl**oo**d	*sh**oo**k	*sch**oo**l
*lettu**c**e	*bl**oo**d		*aftern**oo**n
***c**elebrate	*m**o**nths		
	*n**o**thing		
	*n**o**ne		

*The asterisks indicate the words for Part 2

Fruit Basket Turnover

Make a circle of chairs with each person sitting in a chair except the caller. Each person is secretly given the name of a fruit. Several people are given the same fruit. The caller calls the names of a fruit. The people who have that fruit must exchange seats before the caller gets in their seat or they become the next caller. At any time the caller can say "FRUIT BASKET TURNOVER" and then everyone must find a new seat. Play as long as you like.

A variation is to use the names of vegetables or meats or dairy products instead of fruit. However, stick with one category at a time.

breakfast
dinner
safety
healthy
picnic
biscuits
***ba**con
***sau**sage
***mus**tard
***ketch**up
***yo**gurt

sandwiches
restaurant
cereal
hamburger
cinnamon
***cab**bages
***re**cipes
***typ**ical
***may**onnaise

po**ta**toes
to**ma**toes
ba**nan**as
an **ap**ple
*an **or**ange
*an **on**ion
*some **french** fries
*some **grape**fruit

IDIOMS

● ● ●

Your eyes are bigger than your stomach.
* You are putting too much food on your plate.
You can't eat all of the food on your plate.

● ●

It's
* Something new that
doesn't work very well
or stops working . It
often refers to a car.
This car is a lemon.

● ●

He's putting words in my mouth.
* Answering for someone else.

● ● ● ●

An apple a day keeps the doctor away.
* Eat healthy. If you eat healthy foods, you
won't have to go to the doctor as often.

Part 1

Passover

Moses went back to Egypt. He told the new Egyptian ruler to let the Israelites leave so they could worship God in the desert. The ruler said,"No".

For many months Moses went to Pharoah. The one true God showed His power by performing many miracles.

- The Nile River turned into blood.
- Frogs, stinging flies, and grasshoppers were everywhere and ate the crops.
- Animals died.
- There was a bad hail storm.
- Strange darkness covered the land of Egypt.

All of these things happened to the Egyptians, but nothing happened to the Israelites. Each time something bad happened, Pharoah would not let the Israelites leave.

Definitions:
power - mighty, very strong
performing - doing, action
miracles - something done that cannot be explained by natural means
stinging flies- biting flies
grasshoppers - insects
frogs - amphibians

Discussion Questions:
1. Where did Moses go?
2. What did Moses tell the new Egyptian ruler? Why?
3. What did the ruler tell Moses?
4. What did Moses and God do for many months?
5. What were some of the miracles that God did?
6. Why do you think the bad things happened only to the Egyptians and not to the Israelites?

Part 2

Finally, God told Moses that He would send the Angel of Death to kill the oldest boy in each family. The Jews were to kill a lamb and put the blood on the top of their doorposts. If they obeyed their son would live. If they disobeyed their son would die. The Angel of Death would pass over the houses with blood on the doorpost.

The Jews obeyed God.   All the first born Egyptian boys died, but none of the Jewish boys died. Pharoah finally told Moses and the Israelites to leave Egypt.

The Angel of Death passed over the Israelite families that put lamb's blood on their doorposts. This is called *Passover.* The Israelites celebrate *Passover* every year. They eat special food for dinner: unleavened bread, garlic, onions, bitter herbs, cooked lamb and soup.

Exodus 5-12

Definitions:
finally - in the end

Angel of Death - a special angel who kills

doorpost - the top and sides of the door

celebrate - remember, a special occasion and meal

unleavened - no yeast

garlic, onions - vegetables used for flavoring

bitter - sour taste

herbs - plants used for seasoning

Discussion Questions:
1. Finally, what did God tell Moses?
2. What were the Jews supposed to do?
3. If they obeyed, what would happen?
4. If they didn't obey, what would happen?
5. Did they obey? What happened?
6. What did the Pharoah finally do?
7. What is this called?
8. How do the Israelites celebrate *Passover*?
9. What does this mean to Christians today?

The sacrifice of blood was necessary to pay for sin and disobedience. Discuss how this was a picture of what God would do when He sent Jesus to die on the cross. Close each session with prayer when appropriate. Ask for any prayer requests that your students have.

Conversations

Part 2

At home:
A: Are you going to the market / grocery store?
B: Yes, I am. Do you need anything?
A: Please get some _____. (list of food)

At the market:
A: Excuse me, where can I find the
     ___?
B: The ___ is / are on aisle __.

Discuss the costs of food items. Use local
ads in the newspaper to compare prices.
ex. price per pound

At a restaurant:

A   I would like to order a hamburger. (food)

B.   Would you like something to drink?

A.   Yes, I would like a Coke.

B.   I'll bring that right out.

(Discuss paying the bill and leaving the

   restaurant.)

Have a nice day.

Conversion Tables

1 gallon (gal) = 3.7 liters
1 quart (qt) = .95 liters
1 pint (pt) = .4 liters
1 ounce (oz)= .02 liters

1 cup (c) = 99.3 grams
1 Tablespoon (T) = 6.2 grams
1 teaspoon (t) = 2 grams
1 pound (lb)= 453.5 grams

If you would like more information look at the website www.onlineconversion.com.

market
grocery store
groceries
aisle
  *See the list of food from Part 1
restaurant
menu - Use the menu that you made from Part 1 or get some local restaurant menus.

Play - I Am Going to the Market

Make a circle and the first person starts by saying,
"I am going to the market, and in my cart I put (name a food item)."
The next person says, "I am going to the market and in my cart I put (name the same item and add a new one)."
Each person says the same sentence plus the items mentioned before and then adds a new one. This is a good memory game and vocabulary practice.

Objectives

Students will be able to:

1. Recognize the "Pledge of Allegiance", "Star Spangled Banner" and other national symbols of the USA.
2. Understand some of the laws of the USA (eg. driving laws, family laws)
3. Understand the basic structure of the US government.
4. Describe people and emergency situations.
5. Understand basic safety precautions.
6. Recognize safety and traffic signs.
7. Apply for citizenship
   *Name the basic reqirements to attain US citizenship.
   *Identify at least two basic rights of citizenship.
   *Identify at least two responsibilities of US citizens and compare two responsibilities that everyone has as humans.
   *Identify the documents needed to attain US citizenship.

Materials Needed for Lesson 8

1. Paper and pens
2. Pictures to illustrate all of the vocabulary
3. Pronunciation and Rhythm charts
4. Song chart - "America"
5. Name tags for students and teachers
6. Copy of the "Bill of Rights",
   Driver's Manual,
   Immigration laws
7. Bring safety equipment

8   Laws

Ten Commandments

Part 1
LAWS and PENALTIES

Discuss **immigrations laws** and how to become a citizen.
(Go to gov.com and select citizenship)

Driving laws: Get the local Driving Manual and go over basic traffic laws.

What should you do if you have a wreck in your vehicle?
* Always stop.
* Check to see if anyone is hurt.
* Call 911 to report the accident.
* Show your driver's license, car registration, and proof of insurance to the police.

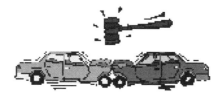

Laws about protection:
You must have a permit to carry a gun. (America)

If you were robbed or attacked how would you describe the person to the police?

height - tall, average, short
weight - thin, medium, fat
hair - brown, black, blond, red, gray
        curly, straight, light, dark
special features - scars, anything
size - large/ small
clothing - teach some clothing here
colors - red, yellow, blue, green, orange, black, white, purple, gray
weapons - gun, knife
transportation - car, van, truck

Laws about children:
* Never leave a child in a car without an adult.
*Never leave children at home alone.

General laws:
Contracts - Be sure to read and understand everything in the contract <u>before</u> you sign it.

Discuss national symbols of the country in which you are teaching: flag, song, capitol city, type of government

The Pledge of Allegiance

I pledge allegiance
I promise to be loyal
to the flag
to our country's symbol
of the United States of America
our country of fifty states
and to the Republic for which it stands
and to the government of our country
one Nation under God,
our country which believes in a higher power,
indivisible
cannot be divided
with liberty and justice for all.
with freedom and fairness for everyone.

American laws and symbols:
Constitution
"Bill of Rights"
"Pledge of Allegiance"
Capitol - Washington DC
Song - "Star Spangled Banner"
Government - Republic

 Practice the Pledge of Allegiance and the Star Spangled Banner with the class.

 **Pronunciation**

Part 1

---

n
nation
penalties
immigration
contract
*citizen
*banner
*indivisible
*united
*knife

---

r
republic
representative
rights
rope
responsibility
*robbed
*recognize
* wreck

---

p
penalties
police
permit
*person
*power
*weapon
*parents
*possibly

---

a (ə)
allegiance
America
adult
alone
*around
*away
*amazed

---

bl
black
blond
blue
blood
*blizzard
*block
*blessed

---

gr
green
gray
grasshopper
grocery
*grapefruit
*great
*ground
* angry

---

er
never
banner
river
higher
driver
*government
*permit
*person

---

o (short u)
person
weapon
protection
registration
transportation
*nation
*Constitution

---

*The asterisks indicate the words for Part 2

IDIOMS:

Don't shoot off your mouth.
* Think before you talk.
* Don't brag.

Bend over backwards
* To go out of your way to help someone

Sell someone down the river
* To betray someone

On ice
* In jail
* To set aside for later use or safekeeping

Get away clean
* To run away without being caught

Jump the gun
* Start too soon

Bible Story

Part 1

Laws

God led the Jews through the desert to the mountain where He first talked to Moses from a burning bush. There were over two million people.

Moses climbed up the mountain and God gave him special commands for the people to obey. God wrote them on stone tablets.

These laws helped people to live the way God wanted them to live.

These are 5 of the 10 Commandments:
1. I am the Lord your God. Worship only Me.
2. Do not make or worship an idol or false god.
3. Do not use My holy [special] name in a wrong way.
4. Keep the seventh day holy (Sabbath).
   Work six days and rest on the seventh day.
   Worship God on this day.
5. Love and obey your father and mother.

Exodus 20

Definitions:

command - to direct with authority, to order someone to do something

commandment - something commanded

mountain - a land mass that is higher than a hill

stone tablets - a flat slab of rock

worship - to honor or reverence as a divine being or supernatural power

Sabbath - the seventh day of the week observed from Friday evening to Saturday evening as a day of rest and worship.

Discussion Questions:

1. Who led the Jews?
2. Where did God lead the Jews?
3. How did God talk to Moses?
4. How many people were with Moses?
5. What did God tell Moses on the mountain?
6. How did God record these special commands?
7. How did these commands help?
8. What are the first 5 of the Ten Commandments?

At the time when God gave the 10 Comandments the Jews were internationals wandering around in foreign countries.

You can use this illustration any time you wish, but you may want to mention that man is sinful and the 10 Commandments show us that we are sinful.

1. God loves you and wants to give you eternal life.

    John 3:16 - "For God so loved the world that He gave His only son that whoever believes in Him will not die, but will have everlasting life."

    Romans 6:23b - "... the gift of God is eternal life through Jesus Christ our Lord."

2. We are separated from God because we are sinful.

    Romans 3:23 - "For all have sinned and fall short of the glory of God."

    Romans 6:23b "...the wages of sin is death."

3. Jesus took our punishment for our sins on the CROSS. When He rose from the dead He showed us that He conquered death.

    Romans 5:8 - "But God demonstrates His own love for us in this: While we were still sinners, Christ died for us."

    John 5:24 - Jesus said,"I tell you the truth, whoever hears my word and believes Him (God) who sent me has eternal life and will not be condemned; he has crossed over from death to life."

4. Ask Jesus to forgive your sin and turn your life over to Jesus to lead you for the rest of your life.

    Acts 10:43 - "All the prophets testify about Him (Jesus) that every one who believes in Him receives forgiveness of sin through His name."

    John 1:12 - "Yet to all who received Him, to those who believed in His name, He gave the right to become children of God."

 Close each session with prayer when appropriate. Ask for any prayer requests that your students have.

Part 2

Laws

Moses led the Jews through the desert to the mountain where God first talked with him. There were over two million people.

Moses climbed up the mountain and God gave him special commands for the people to obey. God wrote them on stone tablets.

These laws helped people to live the way God wanted them to live.

Here are the Ten Commandments:
1. I am the Lord your God. Worship only Me.
2. Do not make or worship an idol or false god.
3. Do not use My holy [special] name in a wrong way.
4. Keep the Sabbath day holy [special].
   Work six days and rest on the seventh day.
   Worship God on this day.
5. Love and obey your father and mother.
6. Do not murder another person.
7. Be faithful in marriage.
8. Do not steal.
9. Do not tell lies.
10. Do not want something that belongs to another person.

These laws still help us today.

Countries use these laws to help rule their people.
Every day these Commandments help us live the right way and obey God.

Exodus 20

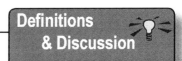

 Act out as many of the words and concepts as you can rather than merely talk about them.

Definitions:

command - to direct with authority, to order someone to do something
commandment - something commanded
mountain - a land mass that is higher than a hill
stone tablets - a flat slab of rock
worship - to honor or reverence as a divine being or supernatural power
Sabbath - the seventh day of the week observed from Friday evening to
          Saturday evening as a day of rest and worship
murder - kill
faithful in marriage - loyal to ones mate, to give allegiance to your mate
steal - to take something that does not belong to you
lie - to tell something that is false

Discussion Questions:

1. Who led the Jews?
2. Where did Moses take the Jews?
3. How did God talk to Moses?
4. How many people were there?
5. What did God tell Moses on the mountain?
6. How did God record these special commands?
7. How did these commands help?
8. What are the Ten Commandments?
9. How do these commandments help people today?
10. Why are the Ten Commandments important?
11. Discuss each commandment and how we break God's laws.

Discuss the fact that everyone is a sinner and deserves judgement.
* Present the idea that God wanted to show how impossible it is to obey the
  10 Commandments and therefore we need Jesus.
* Talk about what Jesus did to satisfy the requirements of the Law.
* Talk about the idea that the sacrifice of blood was necessary to pay for sin
  and disobedience.
* Talk about the Gospel. (See page 105)

 Close each session with prayer when appropriate. Ask for any prayer requests that your students have.

Conversations

Part 2

SAFETY

Discuss safety in each location

At Home

Be careful with fire. (candles, fireplaces, cookers, trash burning)
Never play with matches.
Always keep a fire extinguisher handy.
Install smoke alarms.
Never play with guns or weapons of any kind.
Parents should keep guns locked up.
Put away toys after playing with them.
Keep medicine in a safe place.
Keep cleaning products away from small children.

While Driving

Buckle your seatbelt.
Children should be buckled into a safety seat.
Don't talk on a cellphone.
Don't drink alcohol and then drive.
Obey the driving laws.
Discuss road signs and symbols.

At School

Never take medicine from anyone
except the school nurse.
Tell an adult if anyone threatens you
or anyone else.
Tell an adult if anyone brings a
weapon to school.
Follow school rules about safety.
(sports, labs, field trips)

DANGER

DO NOT ENTER
WITHOUT WEARING
SAFETY GLASSES

At Work

Follow all work related
safety rules.
Operate equipment safely.
Use tools correctly.
Wear protective clothing,
hard hats, and safety
glasses

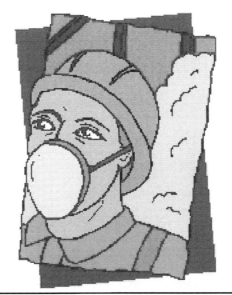

 **Pronunciation**

Part 2

n
nation
penalties
immigration
contract
citizen
*banner
*indivisible
*united
*knife

r
republic
rights
rope
responsibility
robbed
*rules
*rest
*related
*wreck
*wrong

p
penalties
police
permit
person
*power
*weapons
*parents
*possibly

a (ə)
allegiance
America
alone
around
*adult
*available
*apartment
*alarms
*away

bl
black
blond
blue
blood
*blizzard
*block
*blessed

gr
green
gray
grasshopper
grocery
grapefruit
*great
*angry
*ground

-er
never
driver
under
over
power
*order
*higher
*murder
*extinguisher

o (short u)
person
weapon
registration
transportation
nation
Constitution
*million
*mother
*another
*love

IDIOMS:

Face the music.
* To take responsibility for your actions
He made a mistake and now he has to
<u>face the music.</u>

At the end of your rope
* You have done everything that
can possibly be done.
Many bad things had been
happening lately, and you are
<u>at the end of your rope. </u>

Read someone their rights
*When someone is arrested they
are <u>read their rights</u>. "You have the
right to remain silent.

Give it your best shot.
* Do the best job that you can.
You are taking a new class in English,
<u>so give it your best shot.</u>

Objectives

Students will be able to:

1. Describe clothes, sizes, and colors.
2. Understand the concept of credit and the dangers.
3. Shop for clothes
4. Understand the meaning of sales and their value.
5. Know the appropriate clothes for different situations.

Materials Needed for Lesson 9

1. Paper and pens (Sign In chart)
2. Pictures to illustrate all of the vocabulary
3. Pronunciation and Rhythm charts
4. Song chart - The Hokey Pokey
   Head Shoulders, Knees, and Toes
5. Name tags for students and teachers
6. Several "Sale" magazines

9 Clothes

God's
Special Men

Conversations

Part 1

A: Are you going shopping ?
B: Yes. Would you like to come with me?
A.   Yes, I would. Where are you going?
B.   I am going to <u>the Center</u>.
　　　　　　　　(name the store/malls)

The Mall
The Center
Downtown
The Square

Conversations while shopping:

2. A. May I help you?
　　B. Yes, I am looking for a ___ ___. (describe)
　　　　Can you help me find___?
　　　　Where are the _____?
　　　　(No, thank you, I am just looking.)
　　A. Take the ___ to the __ floor.
　　　　Let me show you what we have.
　　　　 We're having a sale on ___.
　　　　Certainly. What size do you need?
　　　　Yes, I would be happy to help you.
　　　　 That ___ looks ____ on you.
　　B. How much is/are the ___?
　　　　How much does this/these _____cost?
　　A. We are running a special on ___?

Have a nice day.

Discuss the wise
use of credit
cards.

114

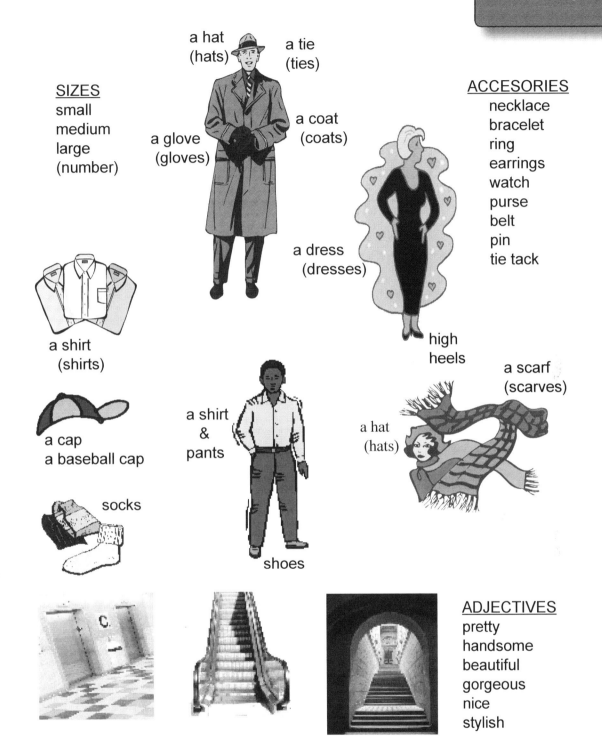

SIZES
small
medium
large
(number)

a hat
(hats)

a tie
(ties)

a coat
(coats)

a glove
(gloves)

ACCESORIES
necklace
bracelet
ring
earrings
watch
purse
belt
pin
tie tack

a dress
(dresses)

high
heels

a shirt
(shirts)

a scarf
(scarves)

a shirt
&
pants

a hat
(hats)

a cap
a baseball cap

socks

shoes

elevator

escalator

stairs

ADJECTIVES
pretty
handsome
beautiful
gorgeous
nice
stylish

 Teach more colors:
Use a box of crayons

Part 1

pr
promise
promised
pretty
protection
products
prove
preparation
privilege
***pr**iests
***pr**ophets

sc (sk)
scarf
scarves
e**sc**alator
school
scars

dr
dress
dressed
drive
drove
***dr**ink
***dr**ank
***dr**y

cl
clothes
client
class
clouds
***cl**oudy
*cir**cl**e

tr
treasure
traffic
trash
true
***tr**opical
*dis**tr**action

sh
shirt
shoes
shorts
shop
***sh**opping
***sh**ow
***sh**ould
*spe**ci**al
*styli**sh**

x (ks)
si**x**
e**x**change
e**x**cept
e**x**cuse
*e**x**plain
*e**x**tinguisher

-tion(shun)
genera**tion**
persecu**tion**
inten**tion**
emo**tion**
ac**tion**
*adora**tion**
*refrac**tion**
*direc**tion**
*sta**tion**

*The asterisks indicate the words for Part 2

Bring advertisments for clothes
and let each student "shop".
Discuss the styles and how
much the clothes cost.

IDIOMS:

● ● ●

Hot under the collar
* Mad, very annoyed

● ●

Up your sleeve
* To plan something secretly

● ●

Lose your shirt
* To lose all of your
money and possessions

● ● ●

The store is running a special.
(The store is having a sale.)

●

In stitches
* To laugh a lot
without stopping

117

Notes

Clothes 9

Part 1

Game: SHOPPING

First person says, " I am going shopping and I put a ___ in my bag."
Second person says, " " " " " " " a ___ and a ___ in my bag."
Third person says,   "   "   " a ___ and a ___and a ___ in my
bag."
Etc. and each person says the things that the others have put in the bag and
then adds one more. It keeps going around the circle until the last person has
had a turn.

Play "Head, Shoulders" (subsitute - head, stomach, arm, leg)
Sing the song as you act out the motions.
*Head, shoulders, knees and toes
                knees and toes
Head, shoulders, knees and toes
                knees and toes
Eyes and Ears and mouth and nose
Head, shoulders, knees and toes

(Substitute other body parts in the song.)

 Act out and discuss as many of the words and concepts as you can rather than merely talk about them. Use the words in sentences and have the students make up sentences as well. Show pictures from the charts.

Part 1

GOD'S SPECIAL MEN

After God led the Israelites to the Promised Land, He chose many special men to lead them and to speak God's words. These men were priests, kings, and prophets. They wore special clothes as a sign of their position.

One of the most famous was King David. God told David that the Promised One, the Messiah, would be a descendent of his family. The Promised One would defeat Satan and rule forever. David was told the Messiah would be called "The Christ", and all nations would be blessed through Him.

Definitions:
Israelites - Jews
Promised Land - Israel
chose - past tense of *choose*
special men - leaders
kings - political rulers
prophets - leaders who tell the future
famous - well known by all
descendent - people who are born after you in your family
defeat - win the battle, conquer

Discussion Questions:

1. Who did God choose to lead the Israelites?
2. What did they wear?
3. Who was one of the most famous leaders of Israel?
4. What did God tell David?
5. Who would the Promised One defeat?
6. What would He do forever?
7. What would the Messiah be called?
8. What would happen to all nations because of the Messiah's coming?

Discuss the connection between these prophecies and sin in "The Fall" from Lesson 3 (page 46).

Haifa

•Nazareth

Sea of
Galilee

Tel Aviv-Yafo

•Bethlehem

JERUSALEM

Gaza

Dead Sea

Be'er Sheva

ISRAEL

Part 2

Another man named Isaiah wrote about "The Christ" and said He would bring God and man back together like they had been before people sinned and disobeyed God. He would die and pay the penalty for all sin. The Christ would be born to a virgin girl in the town of Bethlehem and God would be His father. He said "The Christ" would be called Immanuel which means "God with us". His ministry would begin in Galilee and He would show people how much God loved them by doing many miracles. He would suffer a lot of persecution, and a friend would betray him for 30 pieces of silver. He would be killed by hanging on a tree with wounds in his hands, feet, and side. He would die with criminals, but would be buried in a rich man's grave. Then He would come back to life. He would send the Spirit of God to live inside people who believed Him.

Definitions:
would - conditional verb
sinned - did not obey God
disobeyed - did not obey
penalty - punishment
virgin - never had sexual relations
Bethlehem - a village 5 miles south of Jerusalem
Jerusalem - the capitol of Israel, see the map
Immanual - God with us
Galilee - 50 miles north of Jerusalem, see the map
miracles - supernatural acts
persecution - verbal, mental and physical harm
betray - pretend to be a friend but act like an enemy
criminals - people who commit crimes, disobey the laws
wounds - deep cuts and bruises,
buried - dead body wrapped and put in a cave
come back to life -rise from the dead
Spirit of God - the Holy Spirit

Discussion Questions:
1. Who was another prophet?
2. What would "The Christ" do?
3. What was unusual about His birth?
4. Where would He be born?
5. What would He be called and what does it mean?
6. When would He be announced?
7. Where would His ministry begin?
8. What would He do?
9. What would happen to Him?
10. Who would He send later?
11. Who was born later and fullfilled all of these promises?

These are some prophecies about the Messiah. Use any of them that you wish to reinforce the Bible lesson.

PROPHECIES ABOUT THE MESSIAH'S FIRST COMING

Gen 3:15 Seed of a woman and crush Satan (lesson 1)
Gen 12:7 Special family chosen - Abraham's (lesson 5)
        All nations would be blessed.
Gen 14:18 A priest like Melchizedek
Gen17:19 Seed of Isaac, then Jacob
Gen 49:10 Line of Judah
Ex 12:13 A perfect lamb sacrifice
Ex 12:21 A passover lamb would save
Deu 21:23 Cursed is one who hangs on a tree
2 Sam 7:12 Family of David
1 Chron 17:10-14 A king who would reign forever (Herod tried to kill Him)
Ps. 16:10 Would not see curruption
Ps 22 Details of the crucifiction and resurrection declared
Ps. 45:7,8 Called the Christ
Ps. 72:17 All nations will be blessed thro Him
Is 7:14 To be born of a virgin
Is 9:1,2 Ministry begins in Galilee and identified with miracles
Is 42 Suffering servant
Is 43 He is the only Savior
Is 44 Will send the Spirit of God
Is 53 Describes His death
Dan 9:25 483 years from the order to rebuild Jerusalem He would be announced
Micah 5:2 Born in Bethlehem
Zech 11:12 Betrayed for 30 pieces of silver
Zech 11 & 12 He would be God himself in human form
Job 19:23,27 and Ps.30:3 Resurrection predicted

All 324 of the prophecies
can be found on the website
(www.hopeofisrael.net)

Matthew 6: 28, 33
        Why worry about clothes? Look how the wild flowers grow.
        They don't work hard to make their clothes....Seek first God's
        Kingdom and all these things will be given to you.

1 Tim 6:8 So we should be satisfied just to have food and clothes.

**Conversations**

Part 2

What kind of clothes do I need for ___?
Where did you get ___?
Is that a new ___?
What should I wear to the ___?
How much did the ___ cost?
How many ___ do I need?

Formal Clothes

a bow tie

a tuxedo

an evening gown

high heels

Play Clothes

a tank top

shorts

a shirt

blue jeans

pants

flip flops

Work Clothes

a suit (suits)

uniforms

Fire suit and hat

uniforms

overalls

School Clothes

a backpack

a jacket

a t-shirt

a cap

pants

tennis shoes (sneakers)

jeans

a blouse

a skirt

a purse

a purse

boots

Part 2

pr
promise
promised
pretty
protection
products
prove
preparation
privilege
****pr**iests
****pr**ophets

sc (sk)
scarf
scarves
e**sc**alator
school
scars

dr
dress
dressed
drive
drove
****dr**ink
****dr**ank
****dr**y

cl
clothes
client
class
clouds
****cl**oudy
circl**e

tr
treasure
traffic
trash
true
****tr**opical
distr**action

sh
shirt
shoes
shorts
shop
****sh**opping
****sh**ow
****sh**ould
spec**ial
stylish**

x (ks)
si**x**
e**x**change
e**x**cept
e**x**cuse
ex**plain
ex**tinguisher

-tion(shun)
genera**tion**
persecu**tion**
inten**tion**
emo**tion**
ac**tion**
adoration**
refraction**
direction**
station**

*The asterisks indicate the words for Part 2

IDIOMS:

● ● ●

Keep it under your hat.
* Don't tell anyone, keep it a secret

● ●

Knock someone's socks off
* To really impress someone

● ●

Dressed to kill
* Formal dress/suit
to impress someone

● ●

Spending spree
* To spend a lot of money

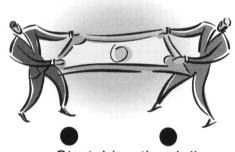

● ●

Stretching the dollar
* Spending your money wisely

● ● ●

Throwing away your money
* Spending your money foolishly

Objectives

Students will be able to:

1. Understand the customs for special days.
2. Understand the significance of Jesus' birth.

Materials Needed for Lesson 10

1. Paper and pens
2. Pictures to illustrate all of the vocabulary
   (Christmas pictures, A wedding magazine &
   any wedding pictures you have to share)
3. Pronunciation and Rhythm charts
4. Song chart - Happy Birthday
   Silent Night
5. Name tags for students and teachers
6. Nativity scene

10
Special Days

Jesus' Birth

Part 1

Discuss/ compare celebrations and gatherings:

Birthdays:

At birthday parties there are special decorations, and the guests give gifts to the one having the birthday. There is a cake with a candle for each year that the person has lived. When the candles are lit the guests sing a song, "Happy Birthday to You", and then the person having the birthday makes a secret wish and tries to blow out all of the candles in one breath. If the person does, the wish is supposed to come true.

How do you celebrate birthdays in your country?

Christenings:

This is a special religious service for a new baby in the family. The purpose is to dedicate the baby to the Lord and the parents vow to raise the child "in the ways of the Lord." Godparents are chosen to help the parents in the raising of this child and a special Christening gown is worn by the baby. Usually a party or reception follows the Christening ceremony.

Definitions:

celebrate (celebrations) - a special way to recognize an event
decorate (decorations) - to put up special things for special occasions or
          holidays

dedicate - to honor someone by giving a pledge or promise
vow - a promise
Godparents - someone chosen by the natural parents to help with the child
   and be responsible if something happens to the parents
reception - a party with refreshments or even a dinner

 Teach the songs -
Happy Birthday
If You're Happy and You Know It

Happy Birthday
Happy birthday to you.(repeat 2 times)
Happy birthday dear _____.
Happy birthday to you.

If Your Happy and You Know It
If you're happy and you know it, <u>clap your hands.</u>(repeat 2 times)
If you're happy and you know it, then your face will surely show it.
If you're happy and you know it, <u>clap your hands</u>

More verses:
If you're happy and you know it <u>stomp your feet.</u>
If you're happy and you know it <u>turn around.</u>
(Add as many more actions as you desire.)

Have a Birthday Party for the students and teachers with cake and
decorations. Give out Birthday cards with each persons birthdate
and appreciation for their hard work.

 **Pronunciation**

Part 1

ar (bar)
party
parties
* Bar Mitzva
*garment
*parchment
*carpenter
*cards

ar (air)
married
marriage
parents
Godparents
*care
*prepared
*necessary

ch (k)
Christening
Christmas
Christian
school
scholar

ing
singing
raising
*gathering
*according
*dancing
*containing
*lasting
*wedding

a (long)
birthday
celebrate
decorate
dedicate
*angel
*lady ladies
*bouquet
*bridesmaid
*Maid-of-
    honor
*veil

u (short)
trusted
but
bunch
young
*supposed
*tuxedo
*couple

i (short)
possible
anniversary
wish
obligation
dedicate
*virgin
*register
*Deliverer
*Genesis

e (short)
engagement
trusted
engaged
expensive
presents
*shepherd
*Bethlehem
*carpenter
*breath
*guests
*Bestman

*The asterisks indicate the words for Part 2

IDIOMS:

Get this show on the road.
* to get started
It's 8:00. Let's <u>get this show on the road.</u>

A wet blanket
* A person who discourages people
Why is he such <u>a wet blanket</u>?

Had a ball
* to have fun
We <u>had a ball</u> at the party.

Party
* To go out and celebrate, have a party
This Friday night we will <u>party</u>.

Different strokes for different folks
* People act differently in different situations
Many people like sports and others like operas.
There are <u>different strokes for different folks</u>.

133

Bible Story

Part 1

Act out and discuss as many of the words and concepts as you can rather than merely talk about them. Use the words in sentences and have the students make up sentences as well. Show pictures from the charts.

Jesus' Birth

At just the right time God sent an angel to tell a young virgin girl named Mary that she was going to have a baby. God would be the father. She didn't know how that was possible, but she trusted God and it happened. The Angel also told Joseph, her fiancé, that this baby would be unique; God in a human body.

Nine months later Mary and Joseph had to go to Bethlehem to register for a census, because they were descendents of David. While they were there the baby was born. The Deliverer promised in Genesis had come. They named Him Jesus, "God who Saves". God chose to announce the birth to some shepherds who were watching their flocks out in the fields that night. Angels filled the skies and told them where to find the baby. They went to Bethlehem to see Jesus and worship Him. Then Mary and Joseph went home to Nazareth.

Taken from:
Matthew 1&2
Isaiah 7:14
Micah 5:2
Isaiah 8:8
1 Chronicles 17:10-14
Jeremiah 31:15
Hosea 11:1
Isaiah 9:1-2

Definitions:

virgin- a woman who has never had a physical relationship with a man
possible- that can be done, could happen, may be
trusted- put your faith in, believe it will happen
fiancé - engaged, promised to marry (In the Jewish culture it was considered
    almost married and could only be broken by divorce.)
unique - one of a kind
register for the census - their names were put on the tax roles
descendents - in the family of
Bethlehem- a small town 5 miles east of Jerusalem
Deliverer - God promised in the Garden of Eden that He would send "the seed
    of the woman" to restore the relationship between God and man
Jesus - God who saves
announce- tell important news
flocks- herds of sheep and goats

Discussion questions:

1. When did God send an angel to Mary?
2. What did the angel tell her?
3. Who would be the baby's father?
4. What did Mary think?
5. Did she trust God? What happened?
6. What did the Angel tell Joseph?
7. Why did Mary and Joseph have to go to Bethlehem?
8. What promise in Genesis had come true?
9. What does Jesus' name mean?
10. To whom did God choose to announce the birth of His son? How?
11. What did the shepherds do?
12. What did Mary and Joseph do?

 Close each session with prayer when appropriate. Ask for
any prayer requests that your students have.

Bible Lesson

Part 2

Jesus' Birth

Later Mary and Joseph went back to Bethlehem and God brought some rich, wise men from the East who were looking for "The King of the Jews". They gave Jesus expensive presents and worshiped Him.

Herod, the governor, tried to kill Jesus by having all of the baby boys in Bethlehem killed. God warned Joseph to leave quickly, and he took Mary and Jesus to Egypt to live for awhile. So Jesus wasn't killed, and when Herod died they went back to Nazareth in Galilee to live.

Jesus grew up there and learned to be a carpenter.

Jesus had different titles: Immanuel - God with us.
                               Christ (Messiah) - Deliverer
                               Jesus - God who Saves

Taken from Matthew 1&2
Fullfilled scriptures:
Isaiah 8:8
1 Chronicles 17:10-14
Jeremiah 31:15
Hosea 11:1
Isaiah 9:1-2

Definitions:

brought - past tense of *bring*
wise - intelligence used in a smart way
East - most likely from Persia
"The King of the Jews" - the future king, Jesus
expensive- costly, worth a lot of money
presents- gifts
worshiped - honored God
Herod - the ruler over Bethlehem in the region of Judea
warned- to tell of something bad that was about to happen
Egypt - a country southwest of Israel
Nazareth- small town in northern Israel where Jesus grew up
grew up - grew from a baby to a man
carpenter- a person who works with wood
titles - names of positions

Discussion questions:

1. What happened later?
2. Who did God bring to Mary, Joseph, and Jesus?
3. Where did they come from?
4. Who were they looking for?
5. What did they give Jesus?
6. What did they do to Jesus?
7. Who was Herod?
8. What did he do?
9. How did God save Jesus' life?
10. Where did Jesus grow up?
11. What skill did He learn?

 **Conversations**

Part 2

 Discuss/ compare celebrations and gatherings:

Special Birthdays
Quincinera:

This is a very special birthday celebrated on the 15th birthday of a young girl. The preparations are elaborate. The celebration traditionally begins with a religious ceremony. A reception is held in the home or a banquet hall. The festivities include gifts, food and music, and dancing.

Bar Mitzva:

A Bar Mitzva celebration is a ceremony that Jewish boys have when they are 13 years old. It is the beginning of a life-long obligation to observe the commandments of the Torah. Similarly, at the age of 12 a Jewich girl becomes Bat Mitzva, which means she is subject to the laws of the Torah that apply to women. There is a religious ceremony and the boy puts on new clothes along with the Tzitzit which is a special garment with fringes on four corners. He also puts on the Tefelin which is a black leather capsule containing the Shema, hand written scriptures on parchment paper, which are tied to his upper arm and head. After the religious ceremony there is usually a dinner party to celebrate the joy of becoming a man or woman in the Jewish community. Gifts are given and there is a lot of singing and dancing.

Funerals:

When a person dies there are many arrangements that have to be made. The body must be taken care of first. Usually a Funeral Home is contacted and they make all of the necessary preparations. A funeral or memorial service is planned and it is usually held in a church or chapel. There are many traditions during the ceremony that depend on the church and family preference. The life of the person is honored and a meal for the family preceeds or follows the ceremony. If the person is buried in a cemetery there is also a short graveside service. People send flowers, food, and sympathy cards to the family to show that they care about them.

Definitions:

preparations - plans, arrangements, gather decorations

elaborate - worked out carefully with great detail

traditionally - according to the customs of the people

reception - a party with refreshments or even a dinner

banquet hall - place where a fancy dinner is served

festivities - the whole celebration

Bar Mitzva - son of the commandment for men

Bat Mitzva - daughter of the commandment for women

obligation - responsible to do somethings

Torah - the Jewish Bible

garment - clothing

fringe - tassels, groups of string

capsule - box

parchment - special long lasting paper

memorial - a symbol to remember someone who has died

sympathy - to show concern, to show that you care

Part 2

 Discuss/ compare celebrations and gatherings:
weddings & anniversaries

Weddings: (American)

The bride is given a promise ring at the time of engagement.

The wedding usually takes place in a church.

The bride wears a white wedding dress & veil.

She has a maid-of-honor and often some bridesmaids.

The groom wears a black tuxedo.

He has a best-man and groomsmen.

Vows are made and rings exchanged and worn on the left hand.

There is usually a reception for the guests after the wedding and the wedding
cake is cut. When the couple gets ready to leave, the bride throws the
bridal bouquet over her shoulder to the single ladies. The lady who
catches it will be married next. The newly married couple then go on a
honeymoon.

What are some of your countries' traditions?

Note: You may teach
passive verb tenses
here.

Anniversaries:

Each year on the same date married couples celebrate their wedding anniversary.
Many times for every 10 years of marriage a party is held. This is especially true
for the 50th anniversary. Many types of parties and sometimes trips are planned
to make the 50th anniversary a unique occasion.

 Have students bring their wedding or
anniversary pictures to share.
Show pictures from BRIDE magazine.

Definitions:

engagement - a man and woman decide to get married

Bride - The bride is the woman who is getting married. In the wedding ceremony she wears a special white dress and veil that represents her purity.

Maid of Honor - The woman that the bride selects to help with the preparations for the marriage. This is usually the best friend or relative of the bride. She comes down the aisle just in front of the bride and stands right beside the bride in the wedding ceremony. She helps handle things such as the bouquet and the ring for the groom.

Bridesmaids - These are good friends or relatives that accompany the bride in the ceremony and help with preparations for the wedding. They wear special matching dresses and come down the aisle just before the bride makes her climatic entrance.

Groom - The groom is the man who is getting married. He wears a tuxedo.

Best Man - This is the best friend or relative of the groom and is charge of helping the groom with preparations for the wedding. He also wears a tuxedo and walks down the aisle with the maid-of-honor and is in charge of the wedding ring for the bride.

Groomsmen - These are friends of the groom who also wear tuxedos and help with the preparations for the wedding. They accompany the bridesmaids in the ceremony.

bouquet - This is an arrangement of flowers carried by the bride. The bridesmaids also carry bouquets.

honeymoon - This is a special trip that is planned for the newly married couple to start the marriage off with joy and a time to be alone.

Part 2

ar (bar)
party
parties
* Bar Mitzva
*garment
*parchment
*carpenter
*cards

ar (air)
married
marriage
parents
Godparents
*care
*prepared
*necessary

ch (k)
Christening
Christmas
Christian
school
scholar

ing
singing
raising
*gathering
*according
*dancing
*containing
*lasting
*wedding

a (long)
birthday
celebrate
decorate
dedicate
*angel
*lady ladies
*bouquet
*bridesmaid
*Maid-of-
    honor
*veil

u (short)
trusted
but
bunch
young
*supposed
*tuxedo
*couple

i (short)
possible
anniversary
wish
obligation
dedicate
*virgin
*register
*Deliverer
*Genesis

e (short)
engagement
trusted
engaged
expensive
presents
*shepherd
*Bethlehem
*carpenter
*breath
*guests
*Bestman

● ○ ○

christening
dedicate
celebrate
Godparents
decorate
different
possible
sympathy
carefully
honeymoon
Bethlehem

○ ● ○

en**gage**ment
ex**pen**sive
ap**pear**ance
re**cep**tion
re**mem**ber
Bar **Mitz**va
ar**range**ments
oc**cas**ions
re**lig**ious

○ ○ ● ○

cele**bra**tion
prepar**a**tion
obli**ga**tion
dedi**ca**tion
Maid-of-**hon**or
decor**a**tion
Happy **Birth**day
situ**a**tion

Objectives

Students will be able to:
1. Discuss different jobs.
2. Locate, or give direction to, common materials and facilities at the work site.
3. Discuss the life of Jesus.
4. Write a resume.
5. Conduct an interview.
6. Deal with bosses and co-workers.
7. Know how to deal with basic work rules and problems.

Materials Needed for Lesson 11

1. Paper and pens
2. Pictures to illustrate all of the vocabulary
3. Pronunciation and Rhythm charts
4. Song chart - "Jesus Loves Me"
5. Name tags for students and teachers
6. Examples of job applications and resumes.

11

Jobs

Jesus' Life

Conversations

Part 1

Tell me about your job.
   What do you do?
   What company do you work for?
   What kind of work do you do?
   What are your responsibilities?
   How many hours do you work?
   What kind of training did you have to get for your job?
   What do you like/dislike about your job?
   How did you get your job?
   Do you want to continue doing this type of work?
      Why or why not?
   Why do you want to speak English better?
   Will it help you with your job?

I am a full time mom.
I take care of my family.

I am a factory worker.
We make ___.

I am a nurse.
  I take care of sick people.

I am a farmer. I grow___.

Jobs:

laborers
nail/hair salon
waitress/waiter
chef/cook
fast food restaurant
dishwasher/bus-boy
bank teller
mechanic's helper
machine shop worker
plumber's helper
landscaping/nursery worker
construction worker
roofer
painter
highway/road worker
factory worker

farmer
food processor
housekeeper
house cleaning
child care worker
salesman/lady
student
professor's assistant
computer worker
call center
seamstress (tailor)
nurse
homemaker
fisherman
custodian
convenience store clerk
cashier

Game- What do you do?

Put the name of a job on each student's back. The students ask questions of each other until they guess the job that is on their back. You can play this game many times.

I am a student.
I am studying ____ at ____(school).

I am a laborer.
I work on ____.

I am a seamstress.
I make clothes.

I am a housekeeper.
I clean houses/ offices.

I am a fisherman.
I catch _____.

I am a construction worker.
I build houses.

I am a waitress.

I am a chef.

We work in a restaurant.

I am a saleslady. We sell_____.

I am a mechanic.
I fix cars.

I am a plumber.
I fix leaking pipes.

Part 1

h
hair salon
helper
highway worker
house cleaning
housekeeper
home maker
*****h**uman
*****h**ealed

c (k)
cook
custodian
construction
computer repair
computer
call center
convenience
cashier
*****c**arpenter
*****c**almed

f
first
factory
farmer
fisherman
fast **f**ood
*****per**f**ect
*****f**ollow
*****f**lesh
*****f**ather
*****in**f**ormation
*****in**f**luence

s
salon
salesman
bu**s**-boy
nur**s**e
seamstre**ss**
waitre**ss**
a**ss**istant
*****wor**s**e
*****S**atan

sh
Engli**sh**
dishwa**sh**er
shop
fi**sh**erman
ca**sh**ier
shape
ship
ma**ch**ine
chef

-d
*****learne**d**
*****starte**d**
*****love**d**
*****baptize**d**
*****raise**d**
*****tempte**d**
*****heale**d**
*****please**d**
*****calme**d**

*The asterisks indicate the words for Part 2

IDIOMS:

● ●
Get the ax
* Lose your job

● ●
Out on a limb
* To take a chance and
help someone

● ●
Don't blow it.
* Don't do something
stupid

● ●
Stick out your neck
* To go out of your way to
help someone

🚲 Teach the song- "Jesus Loves Me"

Jesus loves me this I know
For the Bible tells me so
Little Ones to Him belong
They are weak, but He is strong
Yes, Jesus loves me (repeat 3 times)
The Bible tells me so

Part 1

JESUS' LIFE

As Jesus grew up He learned to be a carpenter, and He dilligently studied God's word. When He was about 30, He started to teach and preach. He started his public ministry by going to be baptized. When He was baptized, God spoke to Jesus and said, "You are my dearly loved son and I am very pleased with you."

Then Jesus went away to be alone and pray. Satan came and tempted Him in 3 ways; desires of the flesh, desires of the eyes, and pride. Jesus didn't do anything wrong. He was the only perfect human.

After this Jesus began to prove that He was God's son by doing many miracles. He healed people from all kinds of illnesses. He miraculously fed thousands of people who came to hear His teaching. He calmed a storm and walked on the water, and He even raised people from the dead.

So many people began to follow Jesus that the Jewish priests were getting jealous. They got so mad that they made plans to kill Jesus.

Jesus taught about God, and many times He used stories to teach lessons. One story was about God the Father. (See "A Father's Love")

Act out and discuss as many of the words and concepts as you can rather than merely talk about them. Use the words in sentences and have the students make up sentences as well. Show pictures from the charts.

Definitions:

dilligently - to work at something with excellence

public - something done where people can see it

baptized - a ceremony that illustrates the washing away of sin

tempted - past tense of *tempt*; to try to get someone to do something wrong

desires of the flesh - anything that affects the body

desires of the eyes - anything that affects what you see

pride - an unduly high opinion of oneself, boastful

miracles - supernatural acts

miraculously - (adverb) describing a miracle

Discussion Questions:

1. What did Jesus learn to do as He grew up?
2. When did He start to teach and preach?
3. How did He start his public ministry?
4. What did God say about Jesus?
5. Why do you think Jesus went alone to pray when He started his ministry?
6. What were the 3 ways that Satan tempted Jesus?
7. How are those things temptations for us?
8. Did Jesus ever do anything that was wrong?
9. Why is that important?
10. How did Jesus show that He was God?
11. Why did so many people start to follow Jesus around?
12. Do we still do that today? Why?
13. Why did that make the religious leaders mad?
14. Why did they want to kill Jesus?
15. Who did Jesus teach about?

 Close each session with prayer when appropriate. Ask for
any prayer requests that your students have.

Conversations

Part 2

Discuss:
How to apply for a green card
(www.usagcls.com)
How to apply for citizenship
(www.uscis.gov)
A job application and a resume
A job interview
How to deal with bosses
How to deal with co-workers
Excellence in your work.

How to write a resume:
There are forms on many programs that you can follow.
Make sure the contact information is very prominent.
List all of jobs you have had and when you were employed.
List all of your education and any extra training.
Make a statement of your job objectives.
Be brief and to the point.

A job interview:
Dress in an appropriate manner for the job to which you are applying.
Smile and give a firm handshake.
Develop a rapport with the interviewer. (Start with light conversation.)
Tell about yourself. (A brief summary of your resume)
Tell about your strengths and how you will help the company.

How to deal with bosses and co-workers:
Always be polite.
Always do your best work.
Get to work on time.
Don't be drawn into arguments.
Correct mistakes as quickly as possible.
Make it clear that your family comes first.

1234 Main Street Anytown, USA   555-555-1234

OBJECTIVE

Write a brief sentence summarizing your goal, the position you are seeking and the kind of place you wish to work.

QUALIFICATIONS & SKILLS

List any qualifications, skills and abilities you have that would set you apart from other people. Mention your dependability and ability to set and meet goals.

EXPERIENCE

2005-2011   (the years you have worked)
List the current or most recent job.

This is the core of your resume. List your jobs chronologically. Start with your current or most recent job. Describe each position you had, your job title, company name and location. State you accomplishments on the job, and your responsibilities. Use action verbs as much as possible.
(Examples:supervised, planned, presented) Be as specific as you can and put in numbers and figures.

2000-2005 Second most recent job
Avoid starting sentences with "I". Use action verbs again, such as, "managed and maintained". Summarize jobs that don't need any explanation.

EDUCATION

List all important degrees and certificates that you have earned. Start with the most recent ones first. Include any "on the job" training that you received on previous jobs.

Pronunciation

Part 2

h
hair salon
helper
highway worker
house cleaning
housekeeper
home maker
*human
*healed

c (k)
cook
custodian
construction
computer repair
computer
call center
convenience
*cashier
*carpenter
*calmed

f
first
factory
farmer
fisherman
fast food
*perfect
*follow
*flesh
*father
*information
*influence

s
salon
salesman
bus-boy
nurse
seamstress
waitress
assistant
*worse
*Satan

sh
English
dishwasher
shop
fisherman
cashier
shape
ship
machine
chef

-d
*learned
*started
*loved
*baptized
*raised
*tempted
*healed
*pleased
*calmed

IDIOMS

● ●

Get the jump on someone
* To get there first, to do something first
She <u>got the jump on him</u>.

● ●

Pull some strings
* To use your influence to get something
He <u>pulled some strings</u> and got a raise in pay.

● ● ●

His bark is worse than his bite.
* He acts like he is angry but he won't hurt you
My boss's <u>bark is worse than his bite.</u>

●

Go to bat
* To support someone

● ●

Shape up or ship out
* Do your job or leave

Bible Story

Part 2

The Story Approach and How to Teach It

Using the **Story Approach** to teach a story is like becoming the director of a play. While you direct the actors to act out their parts, you are teaching them their lines, which includes the story line. This curriculum uses a modified version of the **Story Approach**. Using this approach will enable students to retain up to 90% of the material presented, plus help them to learn how to process it and apply the principles to their own lives.

Teaching "*A Father's Love*":

* Read the story with good intonation and rhythm while showing the illustrations.
* Re-read the story, simultaneously teaching vocabulary in context as you choose students to act out the story, just like teaching a conversation or concept. The vocabulary pages include the definitions and instructions for teaching. If students do not understand, show them what to do, explaining each part by placing students where they need to be. In this way, you will help them define the words themselves.
* Choose people to play the parts while you're reading the story & teaching vocabulary. All students say the sentences as they are being acted out.
* Ask the different questions in the vocabulary sections to establish comprehension.
* Stop occasionally to check comprehension of vocabulary words by having students act out the words or play charades.
* Re-read the story, having all the students saying the sentences with you while the actors continue to act it out. Remember you are a director!
* If students struggle with a particular word, phrase or sentence, say it again and have them repeat it.
* Take all opportunities to have discussions, even limited ones, with the class about the story as you are teaching it.
* Now select students who will perform the parts for a performance. They will need to learn their dialogue as you continue to practice. If your students are capable, have them use the intermediate script noted in the lesson.
* Challenge the students to create appropriate props and attire.
* Select other students to learn the other sentences of the story so the students can tell the story at the performance.
* Practice until the actors can perform the story without help and the class can say the story line together. Another option is to have the actors perform the story with individual students reciting one or two of the story lines each.
* Perform the story using available props and attire.
* Ask the questions in **Discussion** on page 168 and teach the scriptures.

11 Jesus' Stories

A Father's Love

Luke 15:11-32

Once in a faraway land, a man had two sons.

The younger son said to his father, "Give me my share of the property. I'm leaving."   So the father divided his property between his two sons.

1. Once in <u>a faraway land</u>, a man had two sons.

a faraway land--a place, country, a long way from here
had--past tense of *have*
> Have 2 students come to the front to be the 2 sons.
> Get one volunteer to be the father. You may want to have a daughter and a
> > son instead of sons if you have a predominantly female class. You may
> > want to use props, such as hats, shirts or ties to indicate a man or even
> > washable paints or face crayons for a moustache.
> You will want to set up different areas of the room for the different scenes in
> > this story. Have props ready for each area.
> Set this first scene up as the home of the father and sons.
> Have all the students repeat this line.

2. The <u>younger</u> son <u>said</u> to his father, "Give me my <u>share</u> of the <u>property</u>. I'm <u>leaving</u>."

younger--not as old as the other son
said--past tense of *say*
share--part belonging to him as a son; in this case it would be half
property--possessions of the father to which the sons had legal right
> Indicate that one son is older than the other, To indicate that the younger
> > son wants his part of the property, have the son take the play money
> > and say, "This is your property. I want my share, my part." Divide it in
> > two and point to each part and say, "This is one part, one share."
leaving--present continuous of *leave*, which is present of left
> Now have the younger son say his part in sentence #2.
> Have all the students repeat the complete line.

3. So the father <u>divided</u> his property <u>between his two sons.</u>

divided between his two sons--divided is the past tense of divide--separated into
> parts. Here the father separates his money into 2 parts, one part for
> each son. He divides it between the two, which means to measure
> one against the other. The father gave half his money to one son and
> half to the other. If there had been 3 or more sons, he would have
> divided the money "among" the brothers. Between is used only when
> speaking about separating something into 2 parts.
> Take the play money and divide it up into 2 piles.
> Give one to the younger son and keep the other one.
> As you determine how much goes into each pile, tell the students you are
> > dividing the money and it is ***between*** the 2 sons, not ***between*** the son
> > and another person, emphasizing the word ***between***.
> Have all the students repeat the complete line.

Then the younger son packed his bags and took all his money and left home.

The young man wasted all his money on wild living. Soon his money was gone.   The young man had no money for food.

4. Then the younger son packed his bags and took all his money and left home.

packed his bags--past tense of *pack*--put his belongings (clothes and things) in boxes or luggage

took--past tense of *take*--got his possessions.
> Pick up the younger son's share of the money and say, "Took."
> Contrast it with the word "grab" from *Who Is My Neighbor*.
> Demonstrate that "take" is not forceful like "grab" is.

all his money--the total amount; the opposite of none.
> Have the younger son pack his bags, take all his money and leave home.
> Have all the students repeat the sentence.
> Have several students come forward and demonstrate this as everyone says the sentence.

5. The young man wasted all his money on wild living.

wasted--past tense of *waste*-- to use thoughtlessly or carelessly; demonstrate this by giving out the play money to everyone in a careless abandonment.

wild living--living in a wild manner, lacking discipline and control.
> Demonstrate spending excess amounts of money on alcohol and cigarettes and partying with the opposite sex. Use your students to help you with this.
> Then have them demonstrate this as you say it.
> Have the younger son demonstrate this.
> Have all the students repeat the complete line.

6. Soon his money was gone.

Soon--shortly

was gone--past participle of *go*--used up; no longer there.
> Now demonstrate the money "being gone" in a short time (soon).
> Have the younger son act it out as they all say the sentence.

7. The young man had no money for food.

food--something that gives us nourishment, such as fruits and vegetables.
> Have the young man playing this part show that he has no money for food. Show empty pockets or an empty wallet.
> Have him pick up food when he says "food."
> Have the young man demonstrate it again as everyone repeats the line.

No one helped him. Finally he found a job taking care of pigs. He was so hungry he began eating with the pigs. "I'm so hungry! I need some food. I need a job. Why am I eating with the pigs. This is senseless!"

One day he came to his senses. He said, "My father's servants have plenty to eat. I have sinned against God and my father. I'm going home." So the young man went home.

8. No one <u>helped</u> him. <u>Finally</u> he <u>found a job</u> <u>taking care of pigs</u>.

helped--past tense of *help*
finally--occuring at the end, last
found a job--past tense of *find* + a job, work
taking care of pigs--feeding the pigs and cleaning their area
    Have the younger son demonstrate this as everyone repeats the line.

9. He was <u>so hungry</u> he <u>began eating</u> with the pigs.
so hungry--very hungry
began eating--past tense of *begin*--started eating
    Have students act as pigs and have props for food.
    Have the younger son act this out as the students repeat the complete line.

10. "I'm so hungry! I <u>need</u> some food. I need a <u>job</u>."

need-require; act desperate
job--work
    Have the young man act out this part as everyone repeats the dialogue.

11. "Why am I eating with the pigs? This is <u>senseless</u>!"

 senseless--without meaning, foolish
    Have all the students saying the dialogue together while the son acts it out.

12. One day he <u>came to his senses</u>.

came to his senses--past tense of *come*--to become aware of, understand
    Act out an "Aha!" moment and turn away from the pigs.
    Have students also act this out as they say the sentence with you.

13. He said, "<u>My father's servants</u> have <u>plenty to eat</u>.

My father's servants--the employees of the father.
    Ask the students, "Who will be servants for the father?
    Have them stand in the house area.
plenty to eat--lots, enough to eat as one wants.
    Have the servants eat and eat and eat!
    Have the young man say the line as the servants eat. Everyone repeat.

14. I have <u>sinned against God</u> and my father. I'm going home."

sinned against God--past tense of *sin*--an estrangement from God as a result of
       breaking His law
    Have the son showing terrible remorse and sobbing as he acts and speaks.

15. So the young man <u>went</u> home.

went--past tense of *go*
    Have everyone repeat this line.
* Discuss how his heart had changed.

Back home, the father was watching for the younger son.

When the father saw his son, he had compassion. The father ran to him and hugged and kissed him.

16. <u>Back home,</u> the father <u>was watching for</u> the younger son.

Back home--at a former place; in this case, at the house.
>   Have the father standing at the house area waiting for the son, looking for him
>   all the time.

was watching for--past continuous of *watch*--looking carefully and waiting expectantly.
Have the father searching the road for the son, saying,
>   "Where is my son?"
>   Have all the students act out "was watching" as they say it.
>   Have the father act this out as everyone repeats the line.

17. When the father <u>saw</u> his son, he had <u>compassion</u>.

saw--past tense of *see*
>   Have the father show that he saw the son and then act out "had compassion".
>   Continue to have the students saying all the sentences with you as the
>   actors are dramatizing this story. The more the students act and say the
>   sentences the more they will remember and also understand the story.

compassion--deep feelings of pity with a need to show mercy (kindness, forgiveness)
>   Help the students understand what this means. The father was deeply moved
>   by the fact that his son returning and he showed him mercy. He showed
>   him kindness and forgave him.   Discuss forgiveness.
>   To forgive means: to excuse and offense and give up resentment, to cancel
>   payment, to pardon.

18. The father <u>ran</u> to him and <u>hugged</u> and <u>kissed</u> him.

ran--past tense of *run*
hugged--past tense of *hug*----to hold closely in one's arms
>   Hug as many students as you can!
>   Have them demonstrate "hug."

kissed--past tense of *kiss*--touch with the lips
>   Make kissing noises; if appropriate, kiss someone on the cheek or pretend
>   to. Ham it up!
>   Now have the father act the sentence out as you and the others say it.
>   Have different students act out these verbs and verb phrases: ran, hugged,
>   kissed, was watching, came to his senses, was eating, packed his bags,
>   wasted his money, left home, took his money.
>   Tutor, act out these different verbs, nouns and phrases to see if the students
>   can remember the English words for them.
>   Have the students then play **Charades** with the words.
>   Have the father and son act this out as everyone repeats the line.

>   * Help the students understand what this sentence means. When the father
>   ran to him and hugged and kissed him, it indicated that he forgave the
>   son and received him back into the family.

The servants prepared a big feast and everyone began to celebrate, except for the older brother. He was mad and said, "Why are you celebrating for my wayward brother?"

But the father said, "All I have is yours, but it is right to celebrate because, I thought he was dead but he's alive. He was lost and now is found!"

**19. The servants <u>prepared a big feast</u> and everyone <u>began to celebrate</u>,
     <u>except</u> for the older brother. He was mad and said, "Why are you
     celebrating for my <u>wayward</u> brother?'**

prepared a big feast--past tense of *prepare* + a big feast, a big special dinner with
               special food
began to celebrate--past tense of *begin* + to celebrate--start to rejoice; have a good
               time, most likely to have a party
          Everyone act out celebrating. Start to dance, sing and shout.
          Ask them what they are doing, prompting them to say, "Celebrating."
except--but; with the exclusion of--Everyone but the older brother celebrated.
          Ask someone to be the older brother to stand back and act mad.
          Have the actors act this out as everyone says the line.
          * Discuss how the celebration helped to restore the son to the family, and why
          the older brother was mad.
wayward-going the wrong way

**20. The father said, "<u>All I have is yours</u>, but it is right to celebrate because I
     thought he was dead but <u>he's alive</u>.**
All I have is yours-The older son now had all of the inheritance
he's alive--the opposite of he's dead
          This can literally mean that the father now knows his son is not dead because
               he's found him. It is also referencing his spiritual life. It means the
               son is not spiritually destroyed because he came back home, which was
               the right thing to do. It was what God would want him to do.
          Have the actors act this out as everyone says the line.

21. <u>He was lost</u> and <u>now is found</u>!"

he was lost--Literally this means "unable to find his own way; unable to function or
               make progress." Spiritually this means "spiritually destroyed." In this
               story, "He was lost" means both things.
          Help the students understand the literal meaning first: He couldn't find a way
               to make any money. He didn't know where to go as all his so-called
               friends (false friends) had left him. The concept here is that he knew
               where he was physically but not where he was in life; however, the
               feeling was the same.
          Act lost, like you can't figure out where you are.
now is found--Literally, found is the opposite of lost & past tense of find, meaning:
                    1. to come upon after a search and
                    2. to come to an awareness of what one wishes to be and do in life.
          So, the younger son discovers or finds that he is in the wrong place, that he
               went the wrong way in life and now knows what to do--go home.
          Have the actors act this out as everyone says the line.

Definitions & Discussion

Idioms:
  wild living
  jumps for joy
  comes to his senses

Discussion of the main idea:

Who is the story about?
Where was the father?
Where was the older son?
When did this happen?
How did the father feel about giving his younger son his share of
        the property? Why?
What did the young man do with his money?
What happened to the foolish son?
What does 'senseless' mean?
How did the son 'came to his senses'?
What did the son finally realize?
What did he do?
What did he mean by; "I have sinned against God and my father"?
Why had the father been watching for the younger son?
Why did he feel compassion for his younger son?
Why did the father hug and kiss him?
What did the father and the servants do?
How did the older brother feel? Why?
What did he say?
What did his father say?
What do you think he meant when he said;
      "All I have is yours"
        he was dead, but he's alive.
        He was lost and now is found."

What is the story really about? What can we learn from this story?

j
jump
joy
Jesus
Jewish
job
just

a_e
take
place
came
make
gave

i_e
alive
divided
side
time
life
realize

o_e
whole
those
nose
bone
alone
home

wh
why
what
whatever
where
when
which

x
next
except
exit
expensive
exchange

ng
thing
eating
watching
living
giving
celebrating
younger

er
property
servants
younger
later
swerve
older

 Rhythm

● ○ ○
property
everyone
kisses him
celebrate
faraway

● ○ ○ ●
sinned against **God**
thought he was **lost**
sorry for **him**
money was **gone**
plenty to **eat**

● ○ ○ ● ○
took all his **mon**ey
wasted his **mon**ey
came to his **sen**ses
father was **watch**ing
said to his **fa**ther

169

A Father's Love

Once in a faraway land, a man had two sons.

The younger son said to his father, "Give me my share of the property. I'm leaving!" So the father divided his property between his two sons.

Then the younger son packed his bags and took all his money and left home.

The young man wasted all his money on wild living. Soon his money was gone. The young man had no money for food.

No one helped him. Finally he found a job taking care of pigs.
He was so hungry he began eating with the pigs.
"I'm so hungry! I need some food. Why am I eating with the pigs? This is senseless."

One day he came to his senses. He said, "My father's servants have plenty to eat. I have sinned against God and my father. I'm going home."
So the young man went home.

Back home, the father was watching for the younger son. When the father saw his son, he felt compassion. The father ran to him and hugged and kissed him.

The servants prepared a big feast and everyone began to celebrate, except for the older brother.

The father jumped for joy and said, "I thought he was lost but he's alive. He was lost and now is found!"

--Based on Luke 15:11-24

Discussion Questions:

1. Why did the younger son want to leave?
2. How did this make his father feel?
3. How did his brother feel when his brother left home?
4. How did the younger son live at first?
5. What did he do when his money ran out?
6. What made him "come to his senses"?
7. How do you think he felt as he traveled back to his father's house?
8. How did the father feel as he watched for his younger son?
9. How did the father feel about the older son?
10. Why did the father have a celebration when his younger son came home?
11. How did the father show him that he still loved him?
12. What do you think might have happened if the younger son had not come home?
13. How do you think the older son felt when his brother came home?
    (Read the older brother's reaction from the story in the Bible, Luke 15:25-32)
14. Did the younger brother get what he deserved?
15. Does God give us what we deserve?
16. Is there any reason to obey God?
17. How does this story show God's character?

The full story is found in Luke 15:11-32

 Close each session with prayer when appropriate. Ask for any prayer requests that your students have.

Objectives

Students will be able to:

1. Discuss requirements for education and training to get a job or advance in your present job.
2. Communicate effectively with others.
3. Understand who Jesus claimed to be.

Materials Needed for Lesson 12

1. Paper and pens
2. Pictures to illustrate all of the vocabulary
3. Pronunciation and Rhythm charts
4. Local College & Technical Enrollment books

12
Education & Communication

Jesus' Message

Conversations

Part 1

What is your highest level of education?

High School / College
* Freshman
* Sophomore
* Junior
* Senior
Bachelor's Degree
Master's Degree
Doctorate Degree

Questions to Discuss:
1. Why is it important to get an education/training?
2. Why is it important for you to learn English?
3. Are you going to school or taking some training?
4. What school/college/university are you attending?
5. What courses are you taking in college?
   (What courses did you take in college?
6. What is your major?
7. What year are you in school? (see above)
8. What do you plan to do when you get out of school?
   (Expain as much as possible.)
9. Are you taking special training? What kind?
10. Did you learn how to do your work "on the job"?
11. Discuss "on the job" training.
12, Do you work at home?
13. How did you learn the skills that you use to work at home?
14. Discuss homemaking skills. Examples; cooking, washing clothes,
                cleaning, taking care of children, etc.

SCHOOLS

study   university
major   academy
teacher   college
professor   technical schools
student

Technical College
automotive repair
dental assistant
electrician
plumber
brick layer
roofer
builder
air-condition/heating repair
welding
truck driving
beautician
cosmotology
nursing
culinary
legal assistant
computer entry
machinery operator

Use reflective pronouns:

myself
himself
herself
yourself
themselves
ourselves

Examples:
I did the work <u>myself.</u>
He put <u>himself</u> through college.
She worked hard to improve <u>herself.</u>
Did you do the work <u>yourself</u>?
They worked on the project <u>themselves</u>.
We worked by <u>ourselves</u> to finish the job.

Make up more sentences using the reflective pronouns.

Part 1

tr
training
trusted
traditions
traditionally
tree
truth

tion (shun)
communica**tion**
educa**tion**
assump**tion**s
construc**tion**
* posi**tion**
* organiza**tion**
* applica**tion**
* tradi**tion**

v
verbal
in**v**estigate
uni**v**ersity
con**v**ey
voice
* percei**v**ed
* en**v**ironment
* attenti**v**eness
* undi**v**ided
* recei**v**ing

pl
im**pl**ied
please
re**pl**y
ap**pl**ication
* em**pl**oyed
* **pl**anned
* **pl**edge

ly
correct**ly**
honest**ly**
diligent**ly**
dear**ly**
* extreme**ly**
* miraculous**ly**
* real**ly**
* quick**ly**
* unusual**ly**

or
organization
b**or**ing
sh**or**t
imp**or**tant
oral
* ign**or**ing
* flo**or**
* po**or**
* m**or**e
* f**or**
* sophom**or**e

*The asterisks indicate the words for Part 2

Opposites

attentive - distracted

education - ignorance

ask - reply

verbal - silent

divided - undivided

diligent - lazy

receiving - giving

organization - chaos

rich - poor

Part 1

Jesus' Message

God loved people so much that He sent His son (Jesus) to pay for all the sins of mankind. By living a perfect life without any sin Jesus provided a way to bring people and God together again. The payment was Jesus' death and the resurrection was the proof.   God so loved the world that He gave His only son, that whoever believes in Him (turns his/her life over to God) will have eternal life.

Jesus said, " I am the___
*   WORD - He is God's word to us.
*   LIGHT - He showed us what God is like.
*   LIFE   - He came to give us life forever.
*   SAVIOR - He saves us from being separated from God.(John 4:42)
*   BREAD - He gives us everything we need.(John 6:35)
*   LIVING WATER - He sustains us (John 7:38).

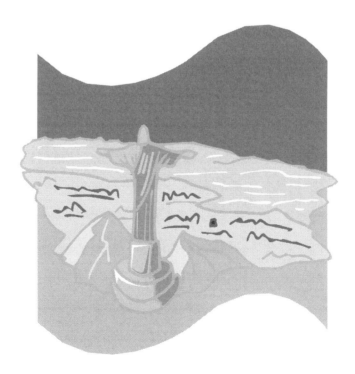

Act out and discuss as many of the words and concepts as you can rather than merely talk about them. Use the words in sentences and have the students make up sentences as well. Show pictures from the charts.

Descriptions:

Word - "In the beginning was the Word ... and the Word became flesh."
(John 1:1,14)

Light - On the first day God created the Light. (Gen.1:3)
"The true light that gives light to every man was coming into the world."
(John 1:1-9)

Life - "...whoever believes in him will not perish but have eternal life."(John 3:16)

Savior - "now we have heard for ourselves, and we know this man really is the
Savior of the World. (John 4:42)

Bread - "I am the bread of life. He who comes to me will never go hungry."
(John 6:35)

Living Water - "If anyone is thirsty let him come to me and drink. Whoever believes
in me ...streams of living water will flow from within him."
(John 7:38)

Discussion Questions:

1. What did God do because He loves people?
2. What did Jesus pay for?
3. How did Jesus live?
4. What did Jesus provide?
5. What was the payment?
6. What was the proof?
7. What do we have to do the have eternal life?
8. Discuss each of the "I am ..."statements that Jesus made.

Close each session with prayer when appropriate. Ask for any prayer requests that your students have.

Part 2

Jesus' Message

God loved people so much that He sent His son (Jesus) to pay for all the sins of mankind. By living a perfect life without any sin Jesus provided a way to bring people and God together again. The payment was Jesus' death and the resurrection was the proof. God so loved the world that He gave His only son, that whoever believes in Him (turns his/her life over to God) will have eternal life.

Jesus said, " I am the___

*   WORD - He is God's word to us.
*   LIGHT - He showed us what God is like.
*   LIFE   - He came to give us life forever.
*   SAVIOR - He saves us from being separated from God.
*   BREAD - He gives us everything we need.
*   LIVING WATER - He sustains us.*
*   GATE - He is the opening to God.
*   GOOD SHEPHERD - He leads us.
*   WAY - He is the way to bring us back to God.
*   TRUTH - He tells us the truth.
*   VINE - He grows us.
*   PEACE - He gives us his peace.
*   MESSIAH - He fullfilled the promises about the "Messiah".

         Taken from the book of John

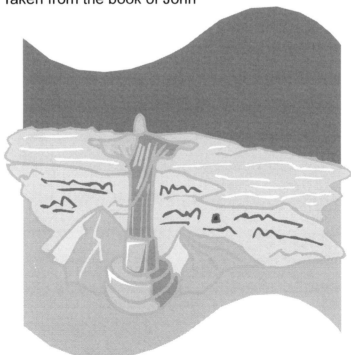

Descriptions:

Word - "In the beginning was the Word ... and the Word became flesh."
(John 1:1,14)
Light - On the first day God created the Light. (Gen.1:3)
"The true light that gives light to every man was coming into the world."
(John 1:1-9)
Life - "...whoever believes in Him will not perish but have eternal life."(John 3:16)
Savior - "now we have heard for ourselves, and we know this man really is the
Savior of the World. (John 4:42)
Bread - "I am the bread of life. He who comes to Me will never go hungry."
(John 6:35)
Living Water - "If anyone is thirsty let him come to me and drink. Whoever
believes in Me ...streams of living water will flow from within him."
(John 7:38)
Gate - "I am the gate. He who enters through me will be saved."
(John 10:9)
Good Shepherd - "I am the good shepherd. The good shepherd lays down his life
for his sheep."   (John 10:13)

Way - "I am the way, the truth, and the life. No man come to the Father except
through me."   (John 14:6)
Truth - " ...grace and truth came through Jesus Christ." (John 1:17)

Vine - "I am the vine; you are the branches. If a man remains in me, he will bear
much fruit; apart from Me you can do nothing." (John 15:5)
Peace - "Peace I leave you. My peace I give to you."   (John 14:27)
Messiah - "But these are written that you may believe that Jesus is the Christ, the
Son of God," (John 20:31)
The woman said, "I know that Messiah (called Christ) is coming.
When He comes, He will explain everything to us." Then
Jesus declared , "I who speak to you am He." (John 4:25 &26)

Discussion Questions:

1. What did God do because He loves people?
2. What did Jesus pay for?
3. How did Jesus live?
4. What did Jesus provide?
5. What was the payment?
6. What was the proof?
7. What do we have to do the have eternal life?
8. Discuss each of the "I am ..."statements that Jesus made.

Conversations

Part 2

COMMUNICATION

Discuss:

What are some ways we communicate?
Why is it important to be able to communicate well?
What can happen if there is miscommunication?
Why is active listening important?
Why is written communication important?
Why is oral communication important?

Communication:
talking
telephone
writing
computer
internet
television
radio
body language
sign language
braille

Tips for good communication

There are 3 parts to a verbal message.
  1. The words that we use must convey our meaning.
  2. The tone of voice is critical.
  3. Your body language is extremely important.
All three parts must align and be consistant for the message to be good communication.

The way a message is perceived is dependent on many factors. There are 2 layers of communication; the **literal** meaning and the **implied** meaning.
The person receiving the message encodes it depending on age, the circumstances, environment, cultural background, personality, feelings, attitudes, assumptions, habits, and past experience.

Use "I" statements rather that "YOU" statements.
  eg. I think...I feel...I see...I understand... instead of
      You think...You feel... You see... You understand...

Don't pretend that you understand what the other person is saying. If you don't understand ask them to clarify it for you. Inquire with open-ended questions if you don't understand. For example, "Please repeat what you said in a different way."

Echo back to the person your understanding of what was said to see if you are receiving the message correctly. "I understood you to say..."

State your message as honestly and clearly as you can in several ways. If you are giving directions or instructions make sure the other person demonstrates there understanding.

Practice active listening. Give your undivided attention to the person who is speaking. Listen with your eyes, ears, and heart. Smile. Affirm that you are listening by nodding your head or leaning toward the person. Touch (if appropriate) and eye contact all convey attentiveness.

Avoid listening barriers.
    *Running Ahead - thinking about what you are going to say
    *Wandering Off - thinking about other things instead of the conversation
    *Jumping In - interrupting the person who is speaking
    *Brushing Away - dismissing the speakers words as unimportant
    *Blocking Out - ignoring what the other person is saying or blocking out parts of it

Part 2

tr
training
trusted
traditions
traditionally
tree
truth

tion (shun)
communica**tion**
educa**tion**
assump**tion**s
construc**tion**
* posi**tion**
* organiza**tion**
* applica**tion**
* tradi**tion**

v
verbal
in**v**estigate
uni**v**ersity
con**v**ey
voice
* percei**v**ed
* en**v**ironment
* attenti**v**eness
* undi**v**ided
* recei**v**ing

pl
im**pl**ied
please
re**pl**y
ap**pl**ication
* em**pl**oyed
* **pl**anned
* **pl**edge

ly
correct**ly**
honest**ly**
diligent**ly**
dear**ly**
* extreme**ly**
* miraculous**ly**
* real**ly**
* quick**ly**
* unusual**ly**

or
organization
b**or**ing
sh**or**t
imp**or**tant
oral
* ign**or**ing
* flo**or**
* po**or**
* m**or**e
* f**or**
* sophom**or**e

*The asterisks indicate the words for Part 2

IDIOMS

● ●

Bury the hatchet
* Quit arguing and work out any differences
that you may have with another person
Let's quit arguing and <u>bury the hatchet.</u>

● ●

Sitting pretty
* You are in a very good position
She just got a raise. She is <u>sitting
pretty.</u>

● ●

Smell a rat
* Something looks wrong
Some money is missing from the
cash register. I <u>smell a rat.</u>

● ●

Sell someone short
* To think a person or thing is
less valuable
He has done a good job, so
don't <u>sell him short</u>.

● ● ●

Feed someone a line
* To lie
He said he owned a movie
company. He was <u>feeding her a line</u>.

Objectives

Students will be able to:
1. Describe a simple illness or injury.
2. Make a doctor or dentist appointment
3. Read and understand emergency words.
4. Know when to call 911 and give the information needed.
5. Read and follow simple directions on medicine labels.
6. Read and report body temperature as indicated on a thermometer.
7. Discuss Jesus' suffering and death.

Materials Needed for Lesson 13

1. Paper and pens
2. Pictures to illustrate all of the vocabulary
3. Pronunciation and Rhythm charts
4. Song chart - "Hokey Pokey"
5. Invite someone in the medical field to come and speak to the class.

13

Health Problems

Jesus' Suffering and Death

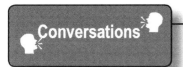

Conversations

Part 1

Health Problems

At home:
    A. What's the matter?
    B. My _____ hurts. (stomach, head, etc)
    A. Let's take your temperature. We'll try __medicine.
        If it isn't better in a few days we will go to the doctor.

At the doctor:
    Patient: I am here to see Dr. Smith.
    Receptionist: Please fill out these papers, and give them to me when
            you are finished.(Discuss how to fill out the medical history.)
    Nurse: (Calls your name.) How are you today?
    Patient: Not too good. (The nurse takes blood pressure and
           temperature.)
    Nurse: Where is the pain?
    Patient: It's here (point to the place that hurts).
           The doctor will be in to see you shortly.
    Doctor: How are you doing?
    Patient: Not very good/well. My ___ hurts.
    Doctor: Let's have a look at you. (Doctor uses his stethoscope.)
          Take a deep breath. Again.
          Does it hurt when I press here?
    Patient: Yes. (No).
    Doctor: Let's take your temperature and blood pressure.
         I think you have <u>an infection</u>.
         Here is a prescription for some medicine.
    Patient: Thank you doctor.
    Doctor: You're welcome. Good-bye.

(Be sure to save the receipt from your doctor to present at work or school.)

 Act out these 2 scenes with your students. Let different
people play the various parts.

If you have a nurse or doctor in your church who may be willing to
come and talk to the students it would be a great asset.

Parts of the Body

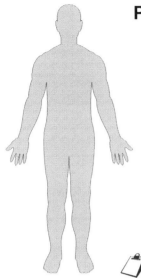

head -eye, ear, nose, mouth, tongue, lips, eyebrows, forehead, teeth, chin, cheeks

neck- throat

arms - shoulders, elbows, wrists, hands, fingers, thumbs

torso - chest, heart, lungs, stomach, belly button, intestines

legs - thighs, knees, shins, ankles, feet, toes

* Practice filling out a health history form (Look in "Filling Out Forms" by New Reader Press.)
* Recognize heath safety signs on meds.
* Practice reading and discuss subscriptions on medice bottles
* Pull to the side of the road for ambulances, police and fire trucks

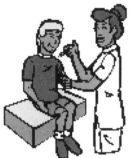

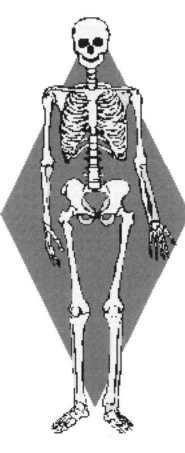

Medicines and tests:
Tylonal (acetaminophen)
aspirin
antibiotic
IV (intravenous)
a shot
blood test
throat culture
x-ray
stress test
CAT scan
exams
take your temperature
take your blood pressure

Illnesses:
infections
a rash
flu
chicken pox
mumps
whooping cough
tetanus
pneumonia
colds
measles
heart attack
high blood pressure
cancer
AIDS
(Auto Immune Diseases)

Part 1

sh	**th**	**ch**	**a (short)**
shin	mou**th**	**ch**in	b**a**ck
shot	tee**th**	**ch**icken pox	scr**a**tch
fini**sh**ed	**th**igh	**ch**eeks	h**a**ve
shortly	**th**roat	**ch**est	st**a**nd
shoulder	brea**th**	*__ch__arged	*h**a**ng
*ra**sh**	*ste**th**oscope	*ri**ch**	*c**a**t
*puni**sh**	*heal**th**		*__a__nxious
*__s__ure	*__th__umbs		*r**a**sh
*pre**ss**ure	*ear**th**quake		

ear	**ow (out)**	**ow (long o)**	**er**
t**ear**	eyebr**ow**	elb**ow**	pap**er**s
h**ear**	d**ow**n	rainb**ow**	ex**er**cise
n**ear**	t**ow**n	foll**ow**ed	fing**er**s
y**ear**	v**ow**	*sh**ow**ed	should**er**
f**ear**	fl**ow**er	*kn**ow**	*matt**er**
		*bl**ow**	*temp**er**ature
			*n**er**ves

*The asterisks indicate the words for Part 2

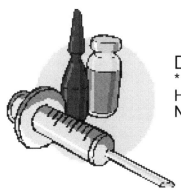

Dose of one's own medicine.
* You get what you deserve.
He always blames others for his mistakes.
Now he is getting a <u>dose of his own medicine</u>.

Get on my nerves
* Makes me irritated, mad
He keeps interupting me. He
is really <u>getting on my nerves.</u>

Get off my back
* Leave me alone
I have apologized and
corrected the mistake I made.
Please <u>get off my back</u>.

Scratch someone's back
* To do something for someone expecting something in return
He did a favor for someone, now he expects them to <u>scratch his back</u>.

Doesn't have a leg to stand on
* Doesn't have any support or factual evidence
She is suing the doctor, but she <u>doesn't have
a leg to stand on.</u>

Under someones thumb.
* to be controlled by someone
He was <u>under his bosses thumb</u>.

All thumbs
* To not be able to do a physical job well
She tried to fix the computer, but she was
<u>all thumbs.</u>

Bible Story

Part 1

Jesus' Suffering and Death

As Jesus became more popular, the "religious" leaders became jealous. They decided to get rid of Jesus by claiming He was breaking the Jewish laws. They charged him with blasphemy, but only the Romans could sentence him to death. So they pressured Pilate, the Roman ruler, into having Him beaten and crucified.

Even as he hung on the cross, He asked God to forgive them. He also asked John to take care of His mother. From noon until 3:00 p.m. it became as dark as night because Jesus was taking our sin on Himself. Then He gave up his spirit and said, "It is finished." Jesus died.

Psalm 22, John 18-19

Act out and discuss as many of the words and concepts as you can rather than merely talk about them. Use the words in sentences and have the students make up sentences as well. Show pictures from the charts.

Definitions:

popular - many people followed Him around
religious leaders - priests of the Jewish religion
jealous - feelings of hatred toward another person
claiming - declaring, stating
charged - made a legal complaint
blasphemy - claiming to be God
sentence - legal term meaning punishment
pressured - influenced
crucified - to kill by nailing a person on a cross (tree)
gave up his spirit - died

Discussion Questions:

1. What did Jesus become?
2. How did the "religious" leaders feel?
3. What did they decide to do?
4. What did they claim that Jesus was doing?
5. What was the charge?
6. What was His final sentence by the Romans?
7. What did Pilate, the Roman ruler, do?
8. What did Jesus ask God to do?
9. Did He do it?
10. What did He ask John to do?
11. What happened at 3:00 p.m.? Why?
12. What did Jesus voluntarily give up?
13. What were Jesus' last words?

 You may want to view the film "The Passion". Close each session with prayer when appropriate. Ask for any prayer requests that your students have.

**Bible
Lesson**

Part 2

Jesus' Suffering and Death

As Jesus became more popular, the "religious" leaders became jealous. They decided to get rid of Jesus by claiming He was breaking the Jewish laws. They charged him with blasphemy, but only the Romans could sentence him to death. So they pressured Pilate, the Roman ruler, into having Him beaten and crucified.

Even as He hung on the cross, He asked God to forgive them. He also asked John to take care of his mother. From noon until 3:00 p.m., it became as dark as night because Jesus was taking our sin upon Himself. Then He gave up His Spirit and said, "It is finished." Jesus died.

At that very moment there was an earthquake and the curtain that covered the "Holy of Holies" in the temple was torn from top to bottom.

Two rich Jewish men came and buried His body in a tomb nearby. The Jewish leaders ask Pilate to put a guard at the tomb and seal it so no one would steal the body, because Jesus told them that He would come back to life again in 3 days.

They thought that they had gotten rid of Jesus for good.

Psalm 22, John 18-19

Definitions:

popular - many people followed Him around
religious leaders - priests of the Jewish religion
jealous - feelings of hatred toward another person
claiming - declaring, stating
charged - made a legal complaint
blasphemy - claiming to be God
sentence - legal term meaning punishment
pressured - influenced
crucified - to kill by nailing a person on a cross (tree)
gave up his spirit - died
earthquake - a natural disaster when the ground shakes
"Holy of Holies" - the most sacred place in the temple, considered to be God's
        throne on earth
tomb - burial place
nearby - next to, close to, in the same area
seal - cover the opening of the tomb with a large rock and put mud around it to
        show if someone moved it

Discussion Questions:
 Review
 1. What did Jesus become?
 2. How did the "religious" leaders feel?
 3. What did they decide to do?
 4. What did they claim that Jesus was doing?
 5. What was the charge?
 6. What was his final sentence by the Romans?
 7. What did Pilate, the Roman ruler, do?
 8. What did Jesus ask God to do?
 9. Did He do it?
 10. What did he ask John to do?
 11. What happened at 3:00 p.m.? Why?
 12. What did Jesus voluntarily give up?
 13. What were Jesus' last words?
 14. What happened in the temple at that very moment?
 15. Who buried Jesus' body?
 16. What did the Jewish leaders ask Pilot to do? Why?
 17. What did they think?

Part 2

In an Emergency:
- A. Is there an emergency?
- B. Yes, there has been _____.(a wreck, a fire, a robbery, etc)
- A. Did you call --------(the police, fire department, 911)?
- B. Yes, the _____(ambulance, fire department...) is on the way.
- A. Is anyone hurt?
- B. Yes. (No.)

(Discuss what to do if you have an emergency situation.)

Discuss Problems:
What should you do if you or someone?
- *got sick/hurt
- *passed out
- *was choking
- *got lost
- *found something
- *were afraid
- *were attacked
- *didn't have a job
- *had no money
- *had no food
- *didn't have a home
- *broke the rules/laws
    or was arrested
- *got a ticket

Emergency:
    Call 911 - State the problem, your location, stay on the phone
                    until help arrives
    CPR - If you are trained in Cardio-pulminary Resuscitation(CPR)
                    and the person has stopped breathing you may want to
                    administer it.
    Driving - pull to the side of the road for emergency
                    vehicles.

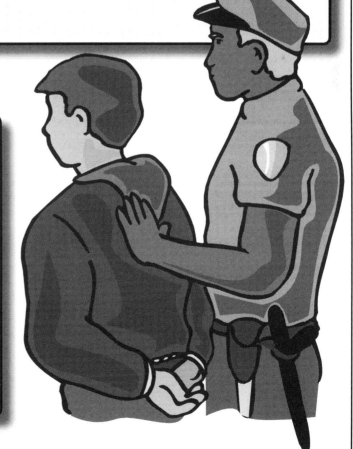

The first ones who help in emergencies are usually family members and friends.

There are many churches and government agencies who will help you in emergencies.

There are shelters and helping organiztions in times of national disasters.

Proverbs 3:7&8

Do not be wise in your own eyes: fear the LORD and shun evil. This will bring health to your body and nourishment to your bones.

Proverbs 10:20

The tongue of the righteous is choice silver, but the heart of the wicked is of little value.

Proverbs 13:3

He who guards his lips guards his life, but he who speaks rashly will come to ruin.

Proverbs 12: 24

Diligent hands will rule, but laziness ends in slave labor.

(25)   An anxious heart weighs a man down, but a kind word cheers him up.

Do the "Hokey-Pokey"

Sing - "Head, Shoulders" (subsitute -other body parts
eg. head, stomach, arm, leg)
Sing the song as you act out the motions.
*Head, shoulders, knees and toes
knees and toes
Head, shoulders, knees and toes
knees and toes
Eyes and Ears and mouth and nose
Head, shoulders, knees and toes

(Substitute other body parts in the song.)

 **Pronunciation**

Part 2

sh
shin
shot
finished
shortly
shoulder
*rash
*punish
*sure
*pressure

th
mouth
teeth
thigh
throat
breath
*stethoscope
*health
*thumbs
*earthquake

ch
chin
chicken pox
cheeks
chest
*charged
*rich

a (short)
back
scratch
have
stand
*hang
*cat
*anxious
*rash

ear
ear
hear
near
year
fear

ow (out)
eyebrow
down
town
vow
flower

ow (long o)
elbow
rainbow
followed
*showed
*know
*blow

er
papers
exercise
fingers
shoulder
*matter
*temperature
*nerves

*The asterisks indicate the words for Part 2

IDIOMS:

● ●
Play it by ear
* Do something that isn't planned
It started to rain so we had to <u>play it by ear</u>.

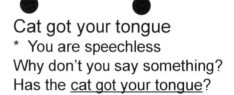

● ●
Cat got your tongue
* You are speechless
Why don't you say something?
Has the <u>cat got your tongue</u>?

● ●
Shoot off your mouth
* To say something that you regret
Don't get mad and <u>shoot off your mouth</u>!

● ● ●
Get in someone's hair
* To bother someone, make them mad
He keeps coming over to my desk. He is
 really <u>getting in my hair</u>.

Objectives

Students will be able to:
1. Describe the holidays and compare the cultural differences.
2. Discuss the events surrounding the resurrection of Jesus.

Materials Needed for Lesson 14
1. Paper and pens
2. Pictures to illustrate all of the vocabulary
3. Pronunciation and Rhythm charts
4. Song chart - "Auld Lang Syne"
        (old time sake)
5. Get the book, "A Look Inside America" by Bill Perry

14 Holidays

Jesus'

Resurrection

Conversations

Part 1

CELEBRATION BOOK

Discussion Questions:
  What holidays do you celebrate?
  When do you celebrate them?
  How do you celebrate?

Discuss the holidays:
  * name the holidays
  * go through a calendar noting when the holiday occurs
  * tell why we celebrate those holidays
  * tell the traditions of those holidays
  * compare & contrast holidays

HOLIDAYS:

New Year
  Most - Jan 1
  Chinese - Feb.
  Jewish - Sept.
  Muslim - Dec.-Jan.
Valentine's Day - Feb.
Easter - March-April
Passover - March -April
Memorial Day - May
Independence Day
  America - July 4
All Hallows Eve - Oct 31
(Halloween)
Thanksgiving - 3rd Thurs. of Nov.
Christmas - Dec 25

Blessed Ramadan

We make/put up decorations.
We invite people to come to our house for a meal.
We give each other presents.
We dress up in our best clothes.
We have a picnic.
We watch/shoot off fireworks.
We go to a worship service at a church, a mosque,
    a synagogue, or a temple.

NEW YEARS DAY

In most of the world New Years Day is celebrated on
January 1st which is according to the Gregorian (solar) calendar.
Other New Years are celebrated on January 14 (Julian calendar). In many Asian
countries it is celebrated between January 21 - February 21 depending on the the
new moon and is generally known as the Chinese New Year. In some countries
New Year comes in March or April, and the Hebrew calendar begins in September.
In most countries people celebrate by having parties and counting down the
minutes until midnight. Many people shoot off fireworks and some give presents.
In China children are given a special red envelope containing money.
Muharram is the beginning of the Islamic New Year, but the date is
different each year because the Muslims use a lunar calendar.

AULD LANG SYNE

Words adapated from a traditional song
by Rabbie Burns (1759-96)

Should auld acquaintance be forgot,
And never brought to mind?
Should auld acquaintance be forgot,
And auld lang syne?

CHORUS:
For auld lang syne, my dear,
For auld lang syne,
We'll take a cup of kindness yet,
For auld lang syne!

Best Answer - Chosen by Asker
Auld Lang Syne" is a song by Robert Burns (1759-1796), although a similar
poem by Robert Ayton (1570-1638), as well as older folk songs, use the same
phrase, and may well have inspired Burns.

In any case, it is one of the better-known songs in English-speaking countries,
and it is often sung at the stroke of midnight on New Year's Day. Like many
other frequently sung songs, the melody is better remembered than the words,
which are often sung incorrectly, and seldom in full.

The song's (Scots) title may be translated into English literally as 'old long
since', or more idiomatically 'long ago', or 'days gone by'. In his retelling of
fairy tales in the Scots language, Matthew Fitt uses the phrase "In the days of
auld lang syne" as the equivalent of "Once upon a time". In Scots Syne is
pronounced like the English word sign — IPA: [sain] — not [zain] as many
people pronounce it.

Part 1

VALENTINE'S DAY

Valentine's Day is a special day to let people know that you love them and is celebrated on February 14. Flowers, candy and other gifts are accompanied by cards that tell the person receiving them that they are special.

EASTER

This holiday, March-April, signals the beginning of Spring and is a day of family gatherings with Easter baskets for the children full of colored eggs and candy. Most families in USA have Easter egg hunts for the children also. For the Christian community it is the highlight of the year, because it is the day that Jesus rose from the dead to become Savior of the world. Many churches have special sunrise services and special dinners with family and friends.

PASSOVER

This holiday is celebrated by the Jews to comemorate when the Death Angel "Passed Over" the Jewish houses that were marked with blood on the doorposts when Jews were in slavery in Egypt. God delivered them out of Egypt and led them to the land of Israel where He gave them the land as their special country.

MEMORIAL DAY

This holiday is a special day to remember those friends and family who have died. We decorate the gravesites with flowers and decorations. We also have special services to remember the soldiers who have fought and died for our country's freedom.

INDEPENDENCE DAY

Almost every country has national celebrations when they gained their independence from an outside government. In the USA we celebrate this day on July 4, because Americans declared their "Independence" from England on that day. (Discuss your students' national holidays that celebrate their freedom that began in their country.)

HALLOWEEN - All Hallows Eve

This is a holiday of fun for children held on October 31. People decorate their houses with jack-o-lanterns, ghosts and goblins. Children dress up in costumes and go from house to house in the evening. They knock on the door and when the person who lives there comes to the door, the children say, "Trick or Treat." The person at the door gives them candy or a treat of some kind. All Hallows Eve is a religious holiday for Catholics to honor their dead relatives and saints. On the night before All Saints Day they clean up the graves of their relatives. Then they put out fresh flowers and lanterns to drive away any evil spirits, and they pray for the people who have died.

 **Pronunciation**

Part 1

ed (d)
baptiz**ed**
sinn**ed**
disobey**ed**
lov**ed**
buri**ed**
*believ**ed**
*fulfill**ed**
*accompani**ed**
*deliver**ed**
*declar**ed**
*cover**ed**

ed (t)
promis**ed**
pass**ed**
announc**ed**
wrapp**ed**
mark**ed**
*thank**ed**
*convinc**ed**
*punish**ed**
*crush**ed**
*drench**ed**
*worship**ed**

ed (ed)
committ**ed**
present**ed**
trust**ed**
want**ed**
educat**ed**
*separat**ed**
*celebrat**ed**
*decid**ed**

in
independence
influence
insurance
infection
instead
***in**structions
***in**vestigate
***in**terview
***in**teresting
***in**divisible
***in**clude

dis
discuss
disaster
discipline
dislike
discourage
***dis**obey
***dis**traction

un
until
unusual
undivided
unleavened
***un**derstanding
***un**important

 Discuss prefixes and suffixes.

*The asterisks indicate the words for Part 2

IDIOMS

Pull someone's leg
* To tease someone
If someone says something that is hard to believe, you say,"You're pulling my leg."

Horse around
* To act silly, physically tease someone
Mothers often say,"Don't horse around in the house. You might break something."

Ratted him out
* To tell about someone who is doing something wrong.
She found out that someone was stealing money from the company, so she ratted him out.

Come alive
* Take something that was very boring and make it spectacular
The movie made the book come alive.

Bible Lesson

Part 1

Jesus' Resurrection

Three days later some of the women who had loved and followed Jesus came to the tomb. They were going to put spices on the body which was the custom at that time. When they got there, the rock that had been in front of the door was rolled away. Two men in shining clothes were there. They said to the women, "Jesus is not here. He has risen from the dead just as He told you."

They were amazed and ran to tell the disciples. Peter and John ran to the tomb to see for themselves, and they found the same thing.

Mary Magdalene stayed at the tomb and Jesus appeared to her and said, "Go tell the disciples I am alive.".

John 20, Acts 1:1-11

Act out and discuss as many of the words and concepts as you can rather than merely talk about them. Use the words in sentences and have the students make up sentences as well. Show pictures from the charts.

Definitions:

resurrection - To be dead and then come back to life
custom - An action that is done as a result of learning from a particular culture
risen - came back to life
amazed - astonished, greatly surprised, awed
Mary Magdalene - A woman who Jesus had helped
appeared - was visible

Discussion:

1. How many days had it been since Jesus was crucified and died?
2. Who came to the tomb first?
3. What were they going to do?
4. What did they see when they got there?
5. What did the angels share?
6. How did the women react?
7. How did they feel?
8. What did the women do next?
9. What did Peter and John do?
10. What did Peter and John find?
11. Who stayed at the tomb?
12. Who appeared to her?
13. How do we know this really happened?

 Close each session with prayer when appropriate. Ask for any prayer requests that your students have.

Bible Lesson

Part 2

Jesus' Resurrection

Three days later some of the women who had loved and followed Jesus came to the tomb. They were going to put spices on the body which was the custom at that time. When they got there, the rock that had been in front of the door was rolled away. Two men in shining clothes were there. They said to the women, "Jesus is not here. He has risen from the dead just as He told you."

They were amazed and ran to tell the disciples. Peter and John ran to the tomb to see for themselves, and they found the same thing.

Mary Magdalene stayed at the tomb and Jesus appeared to her and said, "Go tell the disciples I am alive."

Then that evening Jesus came to the house where the disciples were meeting. He showed them his hands and feet that had the scars from the nails, and He even ate and talked with them.

Over the next 40 days Jesus appeared to many people to prove that he was really alive.

One day as he and the disciples were on a hill Jesus rose into the air. Jesus told them to wait in Jerusalem until the Holy Spirit came to them. Two angels appeared and told them that Jesus would come back to earth again.

John 20, Acts 1:1-11

Definitions:

resurrection - To be dead and then come back to life

custom - An action that is done as a result of learning from a particular culture

risen - came back to life

amazed - astonished, greatly surprised, awed

appeared - was visible

Discussion Questions:
Review

1. How many days had it been since Jesus was crucified and died?
2. Who came to the tomb first?
3. What were they going to do?
4. What did they see when they got there?
5. Who did they see?
6. What did the men say to the women?
7. How did they feel?
8. What did the women do next?
9. What did Peter and John do?
10. What did Peter and John find?
11. Who stayed at the tomb?
12. Who appeared to her?
13. What happened that evening?
14. What did Jesus do?
15. What happened over the next 40 days?
16. What happened one day on a hill?
17. What did Jesus say?
18. What did the angels say?

 How do we know this really happened?
What makes the Bible different from any other religious writings?
Do you think Jesus will come back to Earth someday? Explain.
Does this prove that Jesus is God? How?

Part 2

THANKSGIVING

Thanksgiving is a harvest festival that we celebrate on the fourth Thursday of November. It was first celebrated by the Pilgrims (people from England) and Indians (native Americans) after their first harvest in the New World.

Its purpose is to thank God for providing our food for another year. We have a big family dinner and watch football games. Most cultures have some kind of Harvest Festival. What does your culture do?

Note:
Discuss the difference between the secular and the sacred.
Talk about materialism.

CHRISTMAS

In Christian countries we celebrate a special birthday on December 25. It is Jesus' birthday. We decorate our houses with many things. There is a Christmas tree with lights and ornaments hanging on the branches. We put an angel at the top of the tree to remember the angel's appearance to the shepherds. We put a Christmas wreath on the front door. We buy presents for each other to remember the greatest present ever given to humanity (Jesus), and hang stockings by the fireplace. There are special Christmas programs in all of the churches, and on Christmas day we have a family feast and exchange the presents to show our love for one another.

There is also a custom in many countries that on the night before Christmas a man named Santa Claus comes down the chimney and leaves presents for the children. He puts them under the tree and in the stockings.

Do you celebrate Christmas in your country? What special things do you do?

Thanksgiving words:

Give thanks to God for blessings.
Pilgrims & Indians
turkey & dressing
mashed potatoes & gravy
sweet potatoes
green beans & corn
pumpkin pie
football games
family

Christmas words:

Jesus' birth
Religious programs
Christmas cards
Advent candles
decorations
Christmas tree
wreaths
Santa Claus
North Pole
reindeer
stockings
presents

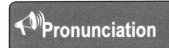 **Pronunciation**

Part 2

ed (d)
baptiz**ed**
sinn**ed**
disobey**ed**
lov**ed**
buri**ed**
*believ**ed**
*fulfill**ed**
*accompani**ed**
*deliver**ed**
*declar**ed**
*cover**ed**

ed (t)
promis**ed**
pass**ed**
announc**ed**
wrapp**ed**
mark**ed**
*thank**ed**
*convinc**ed**
*punish**ed**
*crush**ed**
*drench**ed**
*worship**ed**

ed (ed)
committ**ed**
present**ed**
trust**ed**
want**ed**
educat**ed**
*separat**ed**
*celebrat**ed**
*decid**ed**

in
independence
influence
insurance
infection
instead
***in**structions
***in**vestigate
***in**terview
***in**teresting
***in**divisible
***in**clude

dis
discuss
disaster
discipline
dislike
discourage
***dis**obey
***dis**traction

un
until
unusual
undivided
unleaven
***un**derstanding
***un**important

*The asterisks indicate the words for Part 2

IDIOMS

● ● ●
Kick up your heels
* To go out and celebrate by dancing
Let's go out this weekend and <u>kick up our heels.</u>

●
In stitches
* To laugh for a long time
We laughed and laughed at the comedian. We were <u>in stitches</u>.

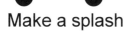

● ●
Make a splash
* To make a very good impression
He really <u>made a splash</u> at the party.

● ● ●
Feel like a million bucks
* To feel extremely good
I finally got over my illness and I <u>feel like a million bucks.</u>

Objectives

Students will be able to:

1. Plan for short and long term goals.
2. Plan a budget.
3. Accept or reject what Jesus said.

Materials Needed for Lesson 15

1. Paper and pens
2. Pictures to illustrate all of the vocabulary
3. Pronunciation and Rhythm charts

15 Plans

Jesus' Return

Part 1

What are your plans for today?
Make a list of things to do tomorrow.
What are your plans for the weekend?
Are you free on Saturday?
How would you like to go _____?

What are your plans for the future?
Are you planning a vacation?
Let's get together and plan _____.
What are you going to do when you finish school?
What are you going to do next week, month, year?

PLANS

calendars, planners
* Get a personal calendar or planner and write down appointments and meetings. Plan for vacations or trips.
* Get a family calendar or planner to keep track of appointments and responsibilites for all family members. Put this calendar in a place where it can be checked easily by all family members.

RECREATION

camping, skiing, swimming, hiking, ball game, sports
Planning for recreation is half of the fun. Make lists of everything you are going to need. Then before you go check your list to make sure you have everything. Keep the list in a handy place so you can add to it when you think of something you are going to need. Often you will have to make reservations. Make sure you take copies of reservation numbers and phone numbers that you may need.

ENTERTAINMENT

movies, games (board), shopping, go out to eat, have coffee
These things don't involve as much planning. If you are meeting someone, make sure the meeting time and place are clearly understood by everyone.

 Plan a social outing together as a class.

Part 1

ex	**-al**	**-ble**
exit	person**al**	a**ble**
except	spiritu**al**	doa**ble**
excuse	education**al**	worka**ble**
exchange	financi**al**	visi**ble**
***ex**plain	natur**al**	possi**ble**
***ex**tremely	*recreation**al**	*valua**ble**
***ex**tinguisher	*festiv**al**	*sensi**ble**
	*tradition**al**	*responsi**ble**
	*physic**al**	*availa**ble**
	*speci**al**	
	*etern**al**	

ä	**ə**	**oi (oy)**
ch**a**rge	**a**mazed	appo**i**ntment
p**a**rtner	**a**stonished	enj**oy**
awed	**a**ppeared	ann**oy**ed
sc**a**rs	**a**ccording	t**oy**s
c**a**lled	**a**ttached	s**oy**
*c**a**rds	***a**rrested	***oi**l
*footb**a**ll	***a**ffirm	*s**oi**l
*h**a**rvest	***a**void	*j**oi**n
*w**a**nted	***a**ttention	*t**oi**let
*m**a**rked	***a**ccount	*c**oi**ns

*The asterisks indicate the words for Part 2

IDIOMS

● ● ● ●

Don't spread yourself too thin.
* Don't try to do too much work
Don't work too much or you will <u>spread yourself too</u> thin.

● ●

Toot your own horn
* to brag about yourself
It is not good to <u>toot your own horn.</u>

● ● ●

Put your money where your mouth is.
* Invest in something you believe in
If you think that is a good investment, <u>put your money where your mouth is.</u>

● ●

Pay through the nose
* Pay too much money
If you buy that car you will <u>pay through the nose.</u>

Bible Lesson

Part 1

God's Plan

After Jesus Christ returned to heaven, His followers went everywhere sharing the good news of the Deliverer. Many people believed Jesus was the Deliverer. Groups of believers met regularly to worship, and became known as Christians. They studied God's Word, sang, prayed, and encouraged each other. God used some of the leaders such as Peter, James, John, and Paul to write much of the New Testament. These Christians established churches in many countries. They are still doing this today.

When Jesus left the earth, He promised to return some day to rule as King. The Bible mentions several things that will happen before Jesus returns.
* deceivers claiming to be Christ
* wars increasing in number
* nations rising against nations
* famines in many countries
* earthquakes in many places
* persecution of Christians
* regathering of the Jews in Israel
* People loving pleasure more than God

After Jesus returns, He will crush Satan in a fierce battle. Everyone will appear before God for judgement. Those who have not believed that Jesus was the Deliverer will be punished forever. Those who have believed will live forever with Christ in God's perfect new heaven and earth.

Act out and discuss as many of the words and concepts as you can rather than merely talk about them. Use the words in sentences and have the students make up sentences as well. Show pictures from the charts.

PLANS:

1. Where did Jesus Christ go?
2. What did His followers do?
3. Did anyone believe them?
4. What name do believers use?
5. What does worship include?
6. How was the New Testament written?
7. What did Christians establish?
8. Name some things churches do.
9. What is Jesus' future role?
10. Name some things that will happen before Jesus returns.
11. What will happen to Satan?
12. Was this promised in the Bible?
13. What is the next event after Satan's defeat?
14. What is the final destiny of man?
15. Do you know what your final destiny will be?

 Jesus has gone to prepare us a place.
      (Matt 24, Mark 13, II Timothy 3:1-4)
    Jesus will return for us. (John 14)
        (Revelation)

    Suggestion to use :
      God's Bridge to Eternal Life by
      Detroit Baptist Theological Seminary.
        (majestic-media.com)

 Close each session with prayer when appropriate.
Ask for any prayer requests that your students have.

Bible Lesson

Part 2

God's Plan

Jesus promised to return to earth some day.   (Acts 1:1-11)
Then He will come to rule as the King of the earth.   (Isaiah 9:7)
The signs of His coming are predicted in the Bible.
These are some of the signs.

> *wars
> *famines
> *plagues
> *earthquakes
> *travel & knowledge greatly increase
> *Israel trampled by Gentles until the time of the Gentiles is fulfilled
> *Israel will become a nation again
> *The Church will be taken up in the air to meet Jesus
> *Tribulation
>> 7 years
>> heavenly signs
>> roaring and tossing of the oceans
>> men's hearts will fail
>> evil world ruler that will demand worship
>> evil world religious leader
>> one world religion

After the Tribulation Jesus will rule the earth for 1,000 years. There will be a final battle against Satan in which he will lose, and then God will judge those who did not accept Jesus' payment for their sin. Then God will create a New Heaven and a New Earth that will last forever. Only those who have put their faith and trust in Jesus will live there.

PLANS:

1. What do you think will happen to you when you die?
2. Do you believe in "God"?
3. What are your thoughts about God?
4. Have you ever read the Bible?
5. Do you believe that it is words from God?
6. Do you think those words are true?
7. Does it affect your life in any way?
8. What do you think about Jesus?
9. Do you think Jesus is God?
10. Do you think Jesus is the ONLY way to God?
11. What does "Jesus is the bridge to God" mean?
12. Do you have any responsibility toward God?
13. Do you think Jesus is really coming back to earth someday?
14. Do you think he will rule the earth someday?
15. Do you think there will be a time on earth like the Tribulation?
16. What will happen after the Tribulation?
17. What will God create?
18. How long will it last?
19. Who will live there?
20. Will you live there forever?

Part 2

GOALS

SHORT TERM	LONG TERM
Personal -	Personal -
* character	* spiritual
* health	* educational
* spiritual	* job
	* family
Family -	* friends
* responsibilities	
* fun	Family -
* health	* spiritual training
* spiritual training	* character training
	* marriage partner
	* health care
	* financial

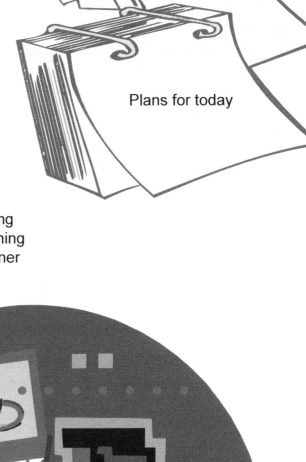

Plans for today

Give students some examples of your goals that you have had and what you did to reach those goals.

Personal Planning

What goals do you have for yourself?
Where would you like to be in 5 years? in 10 years?
What plans do you have to achieve those goals?
Write down some dreams that you have had for yourself.
What would you have to do to get you there?
How long would it take for you to realize those goals?
What are some of your responsibilities now that may or may
    not get in the way of your goals?
Are you willing to do the work and probably the sacrifice that
    it takes to get to your goals?

Financial Planning:

Do you have a plan?

   *Now - What do you have?
   *Future - What do you want to have?
   *Intermediate - How are you going to reach your goals?

BUDGETS

Make a budget based on the plan.
   1. Gather every financial statement you can.
   2. Record all of your sources of income.
   3. Create a list of monthly expenses.
   4. Break expenses in two categories: FIXED & VARIABLE
   5. Total your monthly income and monthly expenses.
   6. Make adjustments to expenses.
   7. Review your budget monthly.

 **Pronunciation**

Part 2

ex
exit
except
excuse
exchange
*__ex__plain
*__ex__tremely
*__ex__tinguisher

-al
person**al**
spiritu**al**
education**al**
financi**al**
natur**al**
*recreation**al**
*festiv**al**
*tradition**al**
*physic**al**
*speci**al**
*etern**al**

-ble
a**ble**
doa**ble**
worka**ble**
visi**ble**
possi**ble**
*valua**ble**
*sensi**ble**
*responsi**ble**
*availa**ble**

ä
ch**a**rge
p**a**rtner
awed
sc**a**rs
c**a**lled
*c**a**rds
*footb**a**ll
*h**a**rvest
*w**a**nted
*m**a**rked

ə
amazed
astonished
appeared
according
attached
*__a__rrested
*__a__ffirm
*__a__void
*__a__ttention
*__a__ccount

oi (oy)
app**oi**ntment
enj**oy**
ann**oy**ed
t**oy**s
s**oy**
*__oi__l
*s**oi**l
*j**oi**n
*t**oi__let
*c**oi**ns

*The asterisks indicate the words for Part 2

IDIOMS:

● ● ●

Take the bull by the horns
* Take charge of your life, take control
<u>Take the bull by the horns</u> and go to school.

● ●

Stick to your guns
* Don't change your mind, continue doing what you are doing
I am sure I am doing the right thing.
I will <u>stick to my guns.</u>

● ● ●

Make ends meet.
* To budget your money so it will pay all of your bills
The increase in taxes will make it hard to <u>make ends meet</u>.

● ● ●

It costs an arm and a leg.
* It costs a lot of money.
The operation <u>cost an arm and a leg.</u>

There are many ways to present the Gospel. Here are some suggested scriptures to use.

1.   God loves you and wants to give you eternal life.

> **John 3:16** - "For God so loved the world that He gave His only son that whoever believes in Him will not die, but will have everlasting life."
>
> **Romans 6:23b** - "... the gift of God is eternal life through Jesus Christ our Lord."

2.   We are separated from God because we are sinful.

> **Romans 3:23** - "For all have sinned and fall short of the glory of God."
>
> **Romans 6:23b** "...the wages of sin is death."

3. Jesus took our punishment for our sins on the CROSS. When He rose from the dead He showed us that He conquered death.

> **Romans 5:8** - "But God demonstrates His own love for us in this: While we were still sinners, Christ died for us."
>
> **John 5:24** - Jesus said,"I tell you the truth, whoever hears my word and believes Him (God) who sent me has eternal life and will not be condemned; he has crossed over from death to life."

4.   Ask Jesus to forgive your sin and turn your life over to Jesus to lead you for the rest of your life.

> **Acts 10:43** - "All the prophets testify about Him (Jesus) that every one who believes in Him receives forgiveness of sin through His name."
>
> **John 1:12** - "Yet to all who received Him, to those who believed in His name, He gave the right to become children of God."

Suggestion to use :
God's Bridge to Eternal Life by
Detroit Baptist Theo.Sem.
(majestic-media.com)

Suggested songs for classes:
1. If You"re Happy and You Know It
2. He's Got the Whole World in His Hands
3. Hokey Pokey
4. Wordless Book Song
5. Jesus Loves Me
6. Jesus Loves the Little Children
7. Head and Shoulders, Knees and Toes
8. God is so Good
9. I've Got the Joy, Joy, Joy, Joy Down in my Heart

If you do not know the tune for these songs, you can go to the following websites to see the words and listen to the tune. Click on the title of the song. This will bring you to the lyrics and then the tune will play.

http://www.kididdles.com/museum/alpha.html
http://www.scoutxing.com/songs/songs.htm

Printed in Great Britain
by Amazon

87275691R00133